RIOT & REVOLUTION

SIR ROBERT GEFFERY 1613–1704

PENELOPE HUNTING

LONDON 2013

PUBLISHED BY
THE GEFFRYE MUSEUM
KINGSLAND ROAD
LONDON
E2 8EA

ISBN 978-1-872828-14-5

DESIGNED BY SALLY MCINTOSH
PRINTED BY HURTWOOD

COVER
Detail from panoramic view of London,
etching by Wenceslaus Hollar, 1647
Detail from Sir Robert Geffery's portrait
by Sir Godfrey Kneller, 1693

SIR ROBERT GEFFERY 1613–1704

CONTENTS

FOREWORD

It is surprising that nobody has written a biography of Sir Robert Geffery before now. He was a prominent figure in seventeenth-century London, a self-made man who rose from a modest Cornish background to the highest positions in the City, weaving his way through the rival factions of Parliamentarians and Royalists, Whigs and Tories, Protestants and Catholics, pursuing a successful career as a merchant and in the process amassing a considerable fortune, most of which he gave to charities. He was a familiar figure to many of the more famous figures of the time, Samuel Pepys, John Evelyn, Robert Hooke, Sir Christopher Wren, as well as the later Stuarts and the infamous Lord Chancellor, Judge Jeffreys. And yet he has remained obscure.

He is remembered principally because of his philanthropy in supporting the school in his birthplace, the village of Landrake in Cornwall and in leaving the largest part of his estate to the Ironmongers' Company to found almshouses. These were duly built in Shoreditch, and were opened in 1714. After almost 200 years they were sold to the London County Council which opened them as the Geffrye Museum in 1914.

This biography has been commissioned by the Geffrye Museum to celebrate the 400th anniversary of Robert Geffery's birth. As an expert in London records and an accomplished historian of City institutions, Dr Penny Hunting was the perfect person to undertake this task. None of us knew what information she might find and it is truly astonishing to see how much evidence she has gleaned from a vast array of sources. We still, sadly, know little about Robert Geffery's character but he achieved greatness in his time and it is good to be able to confirm his place in the history of London.

David Dewing
Director, Geffrye Museum

Sir Robert Geffery's coat of arms, granted by the College of Arms in 1673

ILLUSTRATIONS & SOURCES

ACKNOWLEDGEMENTS

I would like to thank the following for their help, advice and suggestions: Mrs D. Dingle of Tredinnick Farm, Cornwall; Reverend Malcolm Griffiths, Vicar of St Michael's Landrake, and Mr Bob Baldwin, the church's Treasurer, supplied information about the church. Justine Taylor, archivist to the Ironmongers' Company and the Honourable Artillery Company, answered many queries; Leslie Weller gave his expert advice on the paintings and treasures of the Ironmongers' Company and generously supplied several illustrations; Donna Marshall, assistant archivist to the Mercers' Company, helped with Priscilla Geffery's family. Dr Ian Doolittle drew attention to Geffery's properties in Thames Street and Blackfriars Lane. Dr Ann Saunders lent essential books and advised on contacts. Oliver Padel gave me the benefit of his knowledge of Cornish history. Professor Maria Hayward and Dr Nick Karn contributed their Latin expertise, and Nigel Stoughton helped with lexicographical research. Richard Hunting and Sheila O'Connell kindly read and corrected an early draft of the text, and Brenda Herbert tweaked the final version, meticulously. Eleanor John at the Geffrye Museum helped to edit the text and Hannah Fleming was the efficient coordinator of the project. Above all, I thank David Dewing, Director of the Geffrye Museum, for his encouragement, patience and infinite diligence in reading, correcting and re-reading the text.

ABBREVIATIONS

BL: British Library, Euston Road, London

CMIC: Court Minutes, Ironmongers' Company, Guildhall Library, City of London

CRO: Cornwall Record Office, Truro, Cornwall

GL: Guildhall Library, City of London

JE: *The Diary of John Evelyn*, ed. E.S. de Beer (2000)

LMA: London Metropolitan Archives, Northampton Road, London

Nicholl: *Some Account of the Worshipful Company of Ironmongers*, compiled by John Nicholl FSA (1866)

Rep: Repertory (i.e. proceedings) of the Court of Aldermen, City of London, LMA

SP: *The Diary of Samuel Pepys*, ed. Robert Latham and William Matthews (1970–83)

SPD: *Calendar of State Papers. Domestic Series*, ed. F.H. Blackburne Daniell *et al* (1858–1960)

TNA: The National Archives, Kew

NOTE: GEFFERY / GEFFRYE / JEFFREYS

Geffery/Geffrye, Lord Chancellor Jeffreys, the merchants Jeffreys

On his baptism certificate, his will, surviving examples of his signature and in the Repertories of the Court of Aldermen, Robert Geffery's name is spelled Geffery. Some sources adhere to that spelling but variations occur, e.g. Jeffrey/ Gefferey/Gefferyes/Gefferies/Jeffreys/Jeffries/Jefferys/Jeffereys. The Sir Robert Geffery Church of England Primary School, the Geffery Memorial Hall and Geffery Close at Landrake, Geffery's House, Hook, Geffery's Fields, Basingstoke, and Geffery's Court (formerly the Mottingham almshouses, London SE9) are spelled thus, but the Geffrye Museum, Kingsland Road, London E2, differs. The spelling Geffrye crept into use when the Ironmongers' Company set up a committee to administer Sir Robert Geffery's charities after his death in 1704. The minutes of this committee refer to Geffrye's affairs and the planning of Geffrye's almshouses. When the almshouses became the Geffrye Museum under the auspices of the London County Council in 1914 that spelling was confirmed. The same spelling has been adopted for Geffrye Street, Geffrye Court and the Geffrye Estate nearby.

Owing to the variations in the spelling of his name, Sir Robert Geffery has been confused with George Jeffreys, Lord Chancellor of England (1645–89); they were friends. Nor should Sir Robert Geffery be confused with the tobacco merchant John Jeffreys (c.1614–88), a wealthy bachelor who was elected an Alderman in 1660 but paid the fine to be excused. The tobacco merchant's nephews, Alderman Sir Jeffrey Jeffreys (c.1652–1709) and John Jeffreys (c.1659–1715), were friends of both Sir Robert Geffery and Lord Chancellor George Jeffreys.

CHRONOLOGY

| | 1610 | 1620 | 1630 | 1640 |

KEY DATES FOR GEFFERY

1613 Baptism, Landrake, Cornwall

1629 Riot at Landrake Church

1646 Liveryman, Ironmongers' Company

1630 Apprenticeship, Ironmongers' Company
1637 Freeman, Ironmongers' Company

LONDON

NATIONAL AND INTERNATIONAL EVENTS

1625 Accession of King Charles I

1642 First Civil War
1646 Second Civil War
1649 Execution of Charles I

1650

1651 Marriage to Priscilla Cropley
1652 Leases mansion, Lime Street
1653 Membership, Levant Company
1654 Petitioner, East India Company
1655 Constable, Lime Street Ward
1658 Visits Ironmongers' estate, Ireland

1660

1660 Common Councillor, Lime Street Ward
1662 Death of Luke Cropley
1662–7 Deputy Alderman, Lime Street Ward
1663 Exporting cloth to Italy
1665 Importing calico from India
1667 Grant of land, Ireland
1667–8 Master of the Ironmongers' Company
1668 Rebuilds properties, Lime Street,
Thames Street and Blackfriars Lane
1668–76 Deputy Alderman, Lime Street Ward
1669 Purchases land, Cornwall

1670

1670–1 Governor, Irish Society
1670–1 Churchwarden, St Dionis, Backchurc
1672 Charter member, Royal African Compa
1673 Sheriff and knighthood
1673 Leases building plot, Leadenhall
1673–4 Steward, Hon. Artillery Company
1675 Sells land, Cornwall
1676 Death of Priscilla Geffery
1676–1704 Alderman, Cordwainer Ward

1651–4 First Anglo-Dutch war
1653 Oliver Cromwell Lord Protector

1660 Restoration of King Charles II
1665–7 Second Anglo-Dutch war
1665 Great Plague
1666 Great Fire of London
1667 Dutch Fleet in the Medway
1667 Treaty of Breda

1670 Secret Treaty of Dover
1672–4 Third Anglo-Dutch war
1673 Test Act
1678 Titus Oates's Popish Plot

1681 Colonel, City militia
1681 First voyage of the *China Merchant*
1683 Arrested
1683 Assistant, Irish Society
1684 Surrender of Ironmongers' charter
1685 Master of the Ironmongers' Company
1685–6 Lord Mayor of London
1685 Lieutenancy commissioner for the City
1685 Second voyage of the *China Merchant*
1686 Riots, Lime Street 'mass-house'
1687 Dismissed as Alderman
1687 Dismissed, Ironmongers' Court
1688 Reinstated as Alderman
1688 Ironmongers' charter restored
1688 Reinstated, Ironmongers' Court
1689 Third voyage of the *China Merchant*
1689–90 President, Bridewell and Bethlem Hospitals

1700 Leases two properties, Leadenhall
1700 Commands exercise, HAC
1700 Fifth voyage of the *China Merchant*
1702 The Father of the City
1704 February: Death

1712 Purchase of site
for Geffrye Almshouses
1714 Geffrye Almshouses open

1690 Lieutenancy commissioner for the City (renewed 1694)
1691–2 Assistant, Royal African Company
1692 Governor, Tacklehouse Porters and Ticket Porters
1692 Fourth voyage of the *China Merchant*
1693–1704 President, Bridewell and Bethlem Hospitals
1693 Portrait by Kneller commissioned

1690 Anglo-Dutch fleet defeated by French
1694 Bank of England founded
1697 Peace of Ryswyck

1683 *Quo warranto* proceedings
1683 Rye House Plot
1685 Accession of King James II
1685 Monmouth's rebellion
1687 First Declaration of Indulgence
1688 Seven Bishops imprisoned
1688 City's charter restored
1688 November: Prince William of Orange lands, Torbay
1688 December: King James II and Lord Chancellor Jeffreys flee
1689 Coronation of King William III and Queen Mary
1689 Bill of Rights

1701 Act of Settlement
1702 Accession of Queen Anne
1702 War declared on France

1713 Treaty of Utrecht
1714 Accession of King George I

INTRODUCTION

At seven o'clock on the morning of 29 October 1685 the sky was still dark as a multitude assembled outside Ironmongers' Hall on the north side of Fenchurch Street in the City of London. Stout standard-bearers, liverymen in fur-trimmed robes, three dozen trumpeters conducted by a sergeant, and fife-players and drummers wearing crimson and white scarves formed ranks behind the drum-major, all of them shuffled into place by ushers distinguished by their velvet coats and gold chains. The City Marshals were mounted on impatient horses clattering on the cobbles, and a wary Master of Defence kept watch on bystanders, the platoons of pensioners and the sedate figures of the Masters and Wardens of the livery companies who gravitated towards Ironmongers' Hall dressed in their long, warm gowns. Representatives from all echelons of the City gathered this morning to honour Sir Robert Geffery as the ceremonies and festivities surrounding his inauguration as Lord Mayor of London commenced. At Grocers' Hall the procession

swelled with the addition of the outgoing Lord Mayor, Sir James Smyth, and his entourage. Thence to Guildhall where Geffery and his escorts joined the cavalcade. At Three Cranes Wharf, the elite of the City embarked on ceremonial barges which took them upstream to Westminster Hall for the swearing in of Geffery in the presence of the Lords and Barons of the Exchequer. On the return journey to the City the colourful, noisy flotilla streamed past Whitehall Palace, where King James II surveyed the scene apprehensively. The Catholic King, crowned just six months ago, knew full well that the support of the new Lord Mayor was crucial to the survival of the Stuart monarchy.

The Right Honourable The Lord Mayor Sir Robert Geffery, who was to entertain King James, Queen Mary, Princess Anne and Prince George of Denmark, Privy Councillors, Lords of the land and Aldermen of the City at the magnificent dinner that formed the climax to this Lord Mayor's Day, had arrived in London from Cornwall at the age of seventeen. He endured a seven-year apprenticeship and survived Civil War, Cromwell's protectorate, the plague, the Great Fire, the Dutch wars and the absolutist rule of King Charles II to emerge as Master of the Ironmongers' Company, a ship-owner and an overseas merchant dealing in gold, elephants' tusks and enslaved Africans. As Sheriff, Alderman and Lord Mayor of that most ancient municipality, the City of London, Geffery faced grave challenges: riots, rebellion and the revolution that forced King James II and his allies to flee the country. Not for a moment did he falter. A religious man, a merry drinking companion, fair and forthright, Sir Robert Geffery was highly respected by his peers and is still remembered 300 years after his death for his philanthropy, compassion and foresight.

The Lord Mayor's river procession, 1683, British school. Sir Robert Geffery's inauguration as Lord Mayor in 1685 would have been just as splendid

I | A CORNISH BOY

Mr and Mrs Robert Geffery of Tredinnick Farm in south-east Cornwall carried their infant son the short distance from the farmhouse to St Michael's Church, Landrake, for his baptism on 24 May 1613.[1] Family and neighbours gathered around the twelfth-century granite font to witness the vicar trace the sign of the cross on the baby's forehead as he gave him the name of Robert and baptised him in the name of the Father, the Son and the Holy Spirit.

St Michael's Church was – and is – at the heart of the village over which it towers. Rising above the River Lynher, Landrake had once been a Celtic settlement. Known as Landerhtun in 1018, and as Landrei in 1066, the name derived from the Cornish word *lannergh* meaning a clearing. At the time of Robert Geffery's first appearance on the scene, the village was known colloquially as Larrack or Larrick. Small stone cottages straggled along the main street that led to the church, a smithy on one side, the inn on the other. The Gefferys had lived in the area for a century or more: an ancestor called Robert was a landowner of St Antony, downriver from Landrake, in 1522, when three other members of the family lived in the parish of Landrake.[2] Over two dozen men named Gefferye or Jeffrey were listed at a muster of armed villagers of Landrake and neighbouring parishes in 1569,[3] and during the 1620s Robert and Elizabeth Geffery – most likely the parents of Robert – stood at the head of a Cornish family who liked to claim descent from Robert Geffery, Mayor of Trethewy in the late fifteenth century.[4]

The Gefferys were yeomen farmers (as opposed to tenants), the freeholders of Tredinnick Farm in the parish of St Michael's Landrake with St Erney (the tiny sister church was close to the farm). The farmhouse and its outbuildings overlooked fields and streams where sheep, cattle, pigs and poultry were raised and cereals cultivated. A narrow, high-hedged lane passed by the farmhouse, leading to Landrake in one direction and to the church of St Erney in the other. The local vicar was Roger Jope, son and heir of John Jope of Meryfeild, Stokechymsland, Cornwall; the Jopes were gentry and the Reverend Roger, a graduate of Exeter College, Oxford, enjoyed the life of a gentleman farmer.[5] At the time of his death in 1635 he possessed fifty lambs, several horses, a couple of pigs, timber, corn, pewter, books, two fine feather beds, three bedsteads and £40 in gold.[6] His responsibilities to his scattered parishioners were not taxing but would have included instruction of the village children.

With the Bible as the prime text, the children of the parish were taught to read and write and those with application were given access to Jope's library and encouraged to further their education. As the children of a churchgoing yeoman farmer, Robert Geffery and his siblings, William and Thomazin, would have received tuition from Jope, from their mother and perhaps their grandmother at home. Recognising that Robert showed promise and ambition, Jope would have fostered the boy's education and encouraged him to undertake a training that might present wider opportunities than anything Landrake could offer. At a time when some apprentices could not write their own name (those who were illiterate made a mark or finger-print), youths who had the benefit of an education were fortunate and Robert Geffery was grateful for this start in life. When he died at the age of ninety as Sir Robert Geffery, Father of the City of London, his will testified to the importance he placed on the Christian education of children. He made provision for a schoolmaster to 'teach the children of the poore Inhabitants within the parishes of Landrake and St Erney aforesaid to write and read English and to learne and be instructed in the Catechisme now used and appointed in the Church of England'.[7]

THE LOCAL COMMUNITY

The idyllic landscape of south-east Cornwall, the family farm and the support of a closely-knit community formed a solid foundation for the development of young Robert Geffery's fertile mind. Landrake was an isolated village and Tredinnick Farm even more so; the locals relied on the tidal rivers, the estuary and access to the sea to provide the main channels of communication; from the hillside at Tredinnick Robert could watch the boats on the River Tiddy and dream about the world beyond. It is believed that he took a boat on the Tiddy, downstream to the sea, at the start of his journey to London.

There was a weekly market at Saltash (the nearest town, some four miles from Landrake) where supplies could be obtained and produce sold. Landrake itself hosted three annual fairs in February, June and September, which were vital sources for essential goods such as meat, bread, clothing, cider, beer and, of course, for the exchange of news. There were several large farms in the area supporting agricultural workers; local quarries yielded stone and slate for building, while tin-mining had provided employment for generations. Until the dissolution of the monasteries by King Henry VIII, the landowner of Landrake had been the Augustinian Priory of St Germans. Following the surrender of the Prior and half a dozen canons in 1539, parcels of land were acquired by the Eliot family, the Hobarts (inherited by the Edgcumbes), the Maynards and the Carews.

Later in the sixteenth century the plague reached Landrake, claiming fifty-nine victims who were buried in St Michael's Churchyard during the summer of 1593. The early seventeenth century brought poor harvests and a decline in trade which, with the repercussions of war, affected the daily lives of the inhabitants of Landrake, Saltash and the farms and hamlets in the vicinity.

The ports of south Cornwall were well-placed for foreign trade, but the forays of pirates and the threat of invasion by the Spanish were ever-present while Geffery was growing up. Both foreign trade and tin-mining declined from the 1620s; the traditional tin industry, a royal monopoly, suffered from defective organisation and the intervention of outsiders. Tinners, as they were called, earned not more than £4 a year for hard labour in back-breaking conditions and their poverty reached the depths of deprivation in the 1630s. Some tinners turned to agriculture in order to make a living; the agricultural communities of Devon and Cornwall were usually self-sufficient in corn, but in 1622 one storm ruined the entire crop – a local disaster that left families hungry. Shortages of barley were so acute that malt-making was banned in 1623 and 1630, and corn was only available at double its usual price.

Detail from the 'Map of the county of Cornwall newly surveyed by Joel Gascoyne', (1699). Landrake and Geffery's birthplace, Tredinnick, are marked

Francis Drake and the English fleet had famously defeated the Spanish Armada in 1588. The victory was glorious but temporary, and on the death of King James I in 1625 England was again at war with Spain, and this inflicted hardship on the people of south Devon and Cornwall. From the year of Robert Geffery's birth, the mustering of fit young men for military service was compulsory and, in an emergency, youths were forcibly recruited. The outbreak of the Thirty Years War in 1618 increased pressure on the fighting-fit to the extent that those who failed to appear at the local muster or produce adequate arms were hunted down and could be imprisoned. Then, as the country prepared to resume hostilities against Spain in 1625, an armada of 100 ships anchored off the coast, preparing for an attack on Cadiz, and some 300 young Cornishmen were rounded up to fight for their country for 8 pence a day. The massing of an expeditionary force bound for L'Ile de Ré near La Rochelle in 1627, made further demands on Cornish man-power and when the ships returned after a futile attempt to reinforce the French Protestants, they unloaded nearly 5,000 men who were foisted upon households at Landrake and elsewhere at the householders' personal expense and risk. The Mayor of Saltash complained that in the wake of the expedition to L'Ile de Ré, 10,000 men had been billeted in and around Plymouth, with another 2,650 in Cornwall; furthermore, many of the soldiers and sailors were sick, wounded, poorly clothed and undisciplined. An outbreak of the plague was blamed on the infected soldiers and in 1628 martial law was imposed on mutinous servicemen and upon the civilians who housed them. In these circumstances, prospects for the young Robert Geffery of Tredinnick Farm were poor.

UPROAR AT THE CHURCH

The inhabitants of Landrake were discontented and particularly resentful of the government's military impositions, impressments and martial law, as an incident of July 1629 illustrated. Captain Robert Rous of Wotton, brother-in-law of the parliamentarian John Pym, ordered a muster of local men at Landrake Cross, but as the men assembled, a storm broke, so they took shelter in St Michael's Church, which became the backdrop for uproar and violence. One man failed to present the arms required, so was forced out of the church, whereupon his neighbours, led by John Roberts, a gentleman of Landrake and a trained soldier, shouted in protest. Roberts had previously refused to march with the muster and had repeatedly offended the authorities by his 'contemptuous cariage and undecent speaches'. He now emerged as the leader of the protest and he was bold enough to bring legal proceedings against Captain Rous. Roberts's rebellious stance and his incitement of others led to a warrant for his arrest, but the two village constables were his allies and they refused to comply – one of the constables was John Jeffery, surely a relation of the young Robert Geffery (spelling of the surname varied). Consequently Roberts, with constables John Jeffery and Thomas Bake, were ordered to London to be punished for their misdemeanours. The two constables were sentenced to eighteen days imprisonment in the Marshalsea, Southwark. Roberts narrowly evaded a prison sentence but was severely reprimanded and commanded to 'dutifully and dilligently (upon all occasions) attend at the Musters as he ought to doe',[9] 'in that daingerous nooke of the land', Landrake.[10]

One of Roberts's offences had been to hand his pike to a youth to act as his substitute in the muster, and on a second occasion the youth appeared with a broken pike, in an act of defiance. It is tempting to think that this youth was Robert Geffery, who was related to John Roberts and possibly also to constable John Jeffery. If so, might Geffery have seized the opportunity to travel to London with Roberts and the constables (a journey usually made by sea) to support Roberts, and to pursue an apprenticeship? Geffery certainly arrived in London at about this time, and he remained close to John Roberts, who was living at Geffery's house in Lime Street at the time of his death in 1681 and who was buried at St Dionis, Backchurch, at Geffery's behest. His son, John Roberts junior, was taken on as an apprentice by Geffery in 1684 and he remained loyal to his master, ensuring that his wishes regarding a schoolmaster for the children of Landrake were fulfilled – furthermore he married Geffery's niece. This John Roberts was a beneficiary of Geffery's will, as was his aunt, Ann Lower (Miss Roberts of Landrake before her marriage to Thomas Lower MP, of Trelaske, Cornwall, in 1653). Many interesting letters from Robert Geffery were reported to be preserved at Trelaske until at least the mid-nineteenth century, but have since been lost or destroyed.[11]

FROM LANDRAKE TO LONDON

Apart from his family, there was little to keep an ambitious young man like Robert Geffery in Landrake. His father and brother worked the land for a living, but Robert sought his future elsewhere. Robert's first name being the same as his father's indicates that he was the eldest son, so he would have been expected to support his parents in their old age and his sister if she did not marry. As a yeoman's son with some education, the obvious route to prosperity lay through apprenticeship, whereby a good living could be made. It was customary for parents to seek out a master tradesman or artisan to train their son, often applying to a member of the family, a friend or contact in a nearby town or possibly London, which was a magnet for aspiring youths. Dismissing Plymouth, Exeter or Bristol, Robert Geffery and his parents opted for London, where Robert joined hordes of sons of yeomen and husbandmen migrating from the countryside in search of apprenticeships. Not all youths were as successful as Geffery but he was not the only country lad to make his fortune in seventeenth-century London. His career was matched by that of Sir John Moore (1620–1702) from Leicestershire, a Grocer who advanced through the City hierarchy to be Lord Mayor in 1681, and by Sir William Turner (1615–93), who came from Yorkshire, was apprenticed to a Merchant Taylor and elected Lord Mayor of London in 1668. Neither Geffery, Moore nor Turner had any children to inherit their wealth and all three were philanthropists especially concerned with the education of poor children in the counties where they themselves had been born.

The uproar at St Michael's Church, Landrake, in July 1629, and poor prospects in Cornwall generally, presumably persuaded Robert Geffery to leave home and seek an apprenticeship in London. There were several influential figures in and around Landrake who might have steered him in this direction and provided introductions: Sir Richard Carew MP (1579–1643), of the neighbouring village of St Antony, was an educationalist and inventor, and George, Richard, Thomas and Alexander Carew were to be contemporaries of Robert Geffery in the Ironmongers' Company, demonstrating a strong link between this Cornish family and the City Company. Sir John Maynard (1604–90), of Landrake manor and patron of St Michael's Church, was making a name for himself as a lawyer in London and would have been an important contact. Other Cornishmen who had established reputations in London included Sir John Eliot (1592–1632) and Sir Richard Edgcumbe, MP for Cornwall (d. *circa* 1639), but Eliot was in prison from 1628 until 1632, and Edgcumbe had taken the lead in bringing Robert Geffery's relative, John Roberts, to heel after the incident at Landrake church. However Eliot's Deputy Vice Admiral in Devon was Richard Randall whose family had longstanding connections with the Ironmongers' Company. It was with the Master of this Company that Robert Geffery found an apprenticeship – the start of his meteoric career in the City of London.

The Randall family's association with the Ironmongers' Company originated with Justice Randall, who left the Company a legacy in 1585. Another connection was through Thomas Randall of Helston in Cornwall, who married into the Rowe family; Sir William Rowe was Master of the Ironmongers five times and Lord Mayor in 1592. Robert Geffery's sister, Thomazin, married Robert Randall, and several members of the Randall family belonged to the Ironmongers' Company – Richard, William, George, James, Edward and John Randall (a John Randall was Churchwarden of St Michael's Landrake in 1630) were among the fraternity in the second half of the seventeenth century when Robert Geffery was making his mark. Robert and Thomazin Randall, Geffery's brother-in-law and sister, lived at Wandsworth and they may have provided a bed for the eager young man on his arrival from Cornwall (Geffery left £50 to Robert Randall the younger in his will). There were other personal contacts in London who could have helped Robert Geffery: Thomas Opy, for instance, a linen-draper of Bread Street (where the poet John Milton lived with his family at the Sign of The Spread Eagle). Thomas Opy's brother Nicholas and his family were remembered fondly in Geffery's will. There were also several citizens by the name of Geffery/Jeffrey living in the City parishes who might have been related to Robert and offered him encouragement and hospitality when he first arrived in the capital.[12]

Another link between Robert Geffery and the mercantile community of London could have been through Robert Geffreys *(sic)*, who was cited in King James I's charter to merchants of London 'trading into France and the Dominions thereof' in 1611. The subscribers to the French Company included

The Effigies of the right worll. S. James Cambell. Kni. somtime Lo: Mayor. and Senior Aldrn. of London.

Sir James Cambell
was Master of the
Ironmongers' Company
1615–6, 1623–4, 1641–2,
and Lord Mayor 1629–30.
This engraving was
published in 1642

several Masters of the Ironmongers' Company: Nicholas Leate, Sir Christopher Clitherow, Sir James Cambell, Sir Thomas Cambell and Charles Thorold.[13] Ironmongers were also prominent in the affairs of the East India Company during its first decades, when the Ironmongers' Court invested a legacy of £900 with the trading Company. The Robert Geffreys named in King James's charter of 1611 may be the same Robert Jeffries *(sic)*, a Director and Auditor with the East India Company in 1619 and 1621,[14] who was appointed the Company's factor in Persia in 1620. Jeffries/Jefferies was involved in a dispute, dismissed and returned to London where he died in 1623, too early to see Robert Geffery apprenticed.[15] Nevertheless, Clitherow and/or the Cambells, senior figures in the Ironmongers' Company, the East India Company and the French Company, might have persuaded Richard Peate to take on their deceased friend's relative as an apprentice (Sir James Cambell left Peate £100 in his will). By whatever channels Robert Geffery was introduced to Richard Peate, this was a crucial achievement, for once Geffery had secured his apprenticeship with Peate, he could be confident of his future.

APPRENTICESHIP AND FREEDOM

Richard Peate was a stalwart of the Ironmongers' Company who took an active part in its affairs from 1609. He traded in ironmongery and campaigned on behalf of his companions for a good supply of Flemish iron for cutting into rods. There was a shortage of iron in this country, and Peate argued that Flemish iron was of good quality and if it was not imported, the price of home-produced iron would soar.[16] Peate had interests in Bristol (an outlet for pig and bar iron and manufactured ironware from the Forest of Dean and the Midlands) and his visits there surely involved the purchase of ironmongery for sale in London – cutlery, locks, hinges, tools, rods, screws, and nails, which came in 108 different shapes and sizes. Peate was a trading ironmonger; he was never a wealthy merchant or a member of an overseas trading company and he must have been grateful for the bequest left to him by Sir James Cambell in 1642.

Richard Peate, as Senior Warden of the Ironmongers' Company, and Nicholas Leate (1565/6–1631) who was a Past Master of the Company, organised the mayoral pageant for Sir James Cambell in 1629 (Cambell had twice been Master of the Ironmongers' Company). At the close of Cambell's mayoralty, which had been a busy, expensive and high-profile year for the Ironmongers, Peate was elected Master. As such, he was in a position to select apprentices of high calibre and potential, and he recognised these qualities in Robert Geffery. Geffery's apprenticeship commenced with the signing of an indenture promising good behaviour and loyalty to his master and his Company whereby Geffery swore 'to be obedient unto my master by my faith and troth to be unto him in saide matter and to the saide Master and Wardens and commonalty of the Company of Ironmongers of London and to their successors'.[17] Robert's parents paid the apprenticeship fees due to the City Corporation and to the Ironmongers' Company, and a premium in the region of £200 (some £20,000 to £26,000 at 2012 values) to Peate,[18] who acted *in loco parentis* for the ensuing seven years.

Apprentices lived with their master's family, were trained, fed, clothed and strictly disciplined – the Ironmongers' Court of Assistants was particularly averse to apprentices with 'unseemely overlong' hair, which could incur a fine of 20 shillings.[19] Geffery lived with the Peates at Whitecross Street, Finsbury, and would have been set to work doing menial tasks, such as sweeping the warehouse floor and packing, weighing and measuring goods. In his later years as an apprentice he would be promoted to the counting-house to deal with bills, to learn the elements of book-keeping and correspondence and become acquainted with Peate's customers. As Daniel Defoe (1660–1731), a liveryman of the Butchers' Company, pointed out, on completion of his apprenticeship a young man with ambition could 'turn his hand to anything, or deal in anything or everything', having acquired, during the course of his training, a knowledge of goods, places, countries and correspondence.[20]

Robert Geffery completed his apprenticeship with credit in August 1637, whereupon he was 'admitted to the freedom, took his oath and paid the fine' (the fee for not being present on the occasion).[21] The oath of a freeman expressed a lifelong commitment of loyalty to the King and obedience to the Lord Mayor of London. The freeman swore not to trade in foreigners' goods ('foreigners' referred to people from outside London who were not freemen of the City), to uphold responsibilities to apprentices and to abide by the customs and laws of the City (similar vows are taken by today's freemen). At the age of twenty-four, Geffery was now a member of the Ironmongers' Company and a freeman of the City, which gave him certain privileges (the right to drive sheep and cattle over London Bridge, to carry a naked sword in public, to be suspended by a silk rope if hanged and, it is said, to be sent home if found drunk). He was licensed to trade in the City and, as a member of the tenth of the 'Great Twelve' livery companies, Geffery was drawn into a network of merchants who were the life-blood of the City's political and economic health.

In the year Geffery took up his freedom, Izaak Walton (1593–1683) was Warden of the Yeomanry of the Ironmongers' Company, responsible for representing and rallying young freemen such as Geffery. Like Geffery, Walton was a devout Anglican; he was of course senior to Geffery, a married man and a friend of the poet John Donne (1572–1631), whose biography he wrote (Donne's father was a wealthy Ironmonger and a Warden of the Company). Neither Walton's family nor his fellow Ironmongers expected that Izaak's career as a tradesman would be superseded by literary fame – achieved most notably by *The Compleat Angler*, first published in 1653.

Portrait of Izaak Walton (1593–1683), by Jacob Huysmans, *c.*1672. Walton was Warden of the Yeomanry of the Ironmongers' Company when Geffery was a freeman

OPPOSITE
Ironmongers' Hall, Fenchurch Street in the City of London, built in 1587, drawn by 'E.J.G.', *c.*1740

Trained, shepherded and encouraged by Richard Peate and Izaak Walton, Geffery was drawn into the convivial Company of Ironmongers, amongst whom the Thorold family from Lincolnshire was much in evidence, as were the Carews from Cornwall and the Walkers (father and son), while Thomas Heatley, Clerk to the Company for forty years, was its administrative pillar. Thenceforward, Geffery's contemporaries in the Ironmongers' Company were a constant refrain in his life: these were the men he did business with at the Royal Exchange and in the coffee-houses; he conferred with them on Company business, overseas trade and affairs of state, and he dined and drank with them at Ironmongers' Hall.

IRONMONGERS' HALL

Members of the 'Great Twelve' City livery companies are proud of their halls, which signify their status while providing a headquarters for the business of the Company and an impressive setting for social events. The Ironmongers' Company first acquired a hall in 1457, even before it received its charter of incorporation from King Edward IV in 1463. Individual members contributed to the purchase of the property in Fenchurch Street in the parish of All Hallows, Staining, and in Aldgate Ward, within easy reach of Leadenhall, which became increasingly important as a market for ironware, especially nails.

The earliest representation of Ironmongers' Hall, on the copperplate view of c.1553–9, depicts a gabled building on the north side of Fenchurch Street near Billiter Lane.[22] The hall was 'ruinous' and in 'great decay' by 1586, whereupon it was 'new builded' by Elias and Edward Jerman/Jarman, founders of a dynasty of City carpenters (Elias seems to have been the senior of the two).[23] This Elizabethan hall (extended in 1629) was the building Geffery knew, and in 1699 he was on the committee charged with its renovation.[24] An inventory dated 1643, three years before Geffery became a liveryman of the Company,

reveals that it was an imposing edifice, well-furnished, decorated and equipped with items luxurious and essential, from 'cushions of cloth of gould' to barrels of gunpowder. In the great hall where Geffery dined several times each year, members sat at long tables under the gaze of King Charles I, Queen Henrietta Maria and portraits of the Company's benefactors. The armoury was well stocked with pikes, swords, muskets and fifty-eight 'old daggers'. In addition to the court room where Geffery attended meetings for some fifty years, there was a counting-house, buttery, gallery, linen chamber and a 'little house', which stored scales, weights, beams and essential tools of the trade.[25]

The hall completed by the Jermans in 1587 was the home of the Company until the mid-eighteenth century when it was replaced by a classical building designed by Thomas Holden between 1745 and 1750. After bomb damage to that hall in 1917 the Ironmongers moved from Fenchurch Street to Aldersgate Street, where their new hall was built by the Company's surveyor, Sydney Tatchell (1923–5). It survived the Blitz and the development of the Barbican that threatened to engulf it, and continues to fulfil its traditional function.

The Elizabethan Ironmongers' Hall was central to Geffery's career, social life and wellbeing. It was the equivalent of a club-house for trading Ironmongers and increasingly in Geffery's time, a meeting-place for City merchants amongst whom Ironmongers were prominent. The hall was prestigious, and membership of the Company gave Geffery an identity, a position in the City's commercial network and its social hierarchy and provided an entrée into City politics. He could be sure of charitable support from the Company if needed, a decent burial, and trustees who would carry out his wishes after his death.

Once committed to a long and tough apprenticeship, the likelihood of Robert Geffery's return to Cornwall receded. His commitment to a career in the City of London was strengthened by his marriage in 1651 to a London Mercer's daughter, and by his subsequent immersion in the politics, trade and social life of the City. However he did not forsake his home county nor his Cornish relatives: several nieces and their children were remembered in his will. Geffery remained particularly close to John Roberts of Landrake; he counselled his cousin, the widowed Ann Lower (née Roberts) when she needed advice about a property deal in Cornwall, and he left bequests to her and her family. Three of Geffery's eleven apprentices came from Devon or Cornwall, and he acquired property near his birthplace from Richard Rowe, a London merchant, in 1669 for £755;[26] he also owned land at East Wighill until he sold it to Sir Richard Edgcumbe, in 1675.[27] Furthermore, Geffery's will of 1704 told of his lifelong concern for the poor people of Landrake and St Erney, who were to be given bread every Sunday after church and whose children were to be provided with a schoolmaster.[28]

ENDNOTES

1 Baptism certificate of Roberte Geffery, P106/1/1, p.9, CRO **2** T.L. Stoate, *The Cornwall Military Survey, 1522* (1987), pp.99, 106–7 **3** *Cornwall Muster Roll of 1569*, ed. H.L. Douch (1984), p.54 **4** In 1628 and 1629 Robert and Elizabeth Geffery/Jeffery of Landrake are listed by E.A. Fry (ed.), in *Calendar of Wills and Administrations relating to the Counties of Devon and Cornwall proved in the Consistory Court of the Bishop of Exeter 1532–1800*, Index Library (1914), vol 46, pp.82, 112. Unfortunately the documents referred to in this volume were destroyed by bombing in the second world war. Geffery, Mayor of Trethewy in the reign of Edward IV, is referred to in J.L. Vivian and H.H. Drake (eds.), *Herald's Visitation of Cornwall 1620*, Harleian Society (1874), vol 9, p.237 **5** *Herald's Visitation of Cornwall*, op. cit., p.108 **6** Mary Coate, *Cornwall in the Great Civil War and Interregnum* (1933), p.329 **7** Robert Geffery's will, 10 February 1704, PRO/PROB11/475, TNA **8** Anne Duffin, *Faction and faith: politics and religion of the Cornish gentry before the Civil War* (1996), p.123 **9** *Acts of the Privy Council of England May 1629–May 1630* (1960), pp.379–80 **10** Anne Duffin, op. cit. **11** J. Polsue, *Complete Parochial History of Cornwall* (1868), rev. edn. 1974, vol II, p.397 **12** T.C. Dale, *The Inhabitants of London in 1638* (1931) **13** Cecil T. Carr (ed.), *Select Charters of Trading Companies 1530–1707* (1913), pp.62–78 **14** Indexed List of Directors, East India Company, IOR/H/764, BL **15** *Calendar of State Papers Colonial. East Indies 1617–20*, ed. by W. Noel Sainsbury (1870), and Ibid., *1622–24* (1878). Variations in the spelling of Jeffreys/Geffery/Gefferys/Jeoffreyes/Geoffrays makes it difficult to identify individuals who may or may not have been related to Robert Geffery. In addition to the Robert Geffreys who belonged to the French Company (possibly the Geffryes/Jeffries who died in 1623), a Robert Jeoffreys *(sic)* petitioned the East India Company to be employed to oversee the dyeing and dressing of cloth in 1625 and was elected to one of the Company's committees in 1627, see *Calendar of State Papers Colonial. East Indies 1625–27*, op. cit., pp.51, 364, and Court Minutes, East India Company, 4 July 1627, IOR/B/12, BL. This was probably the same Robert Jeoffreyes/Jeffreys/Geoffrays who was born in Wales, served as Master of the Haberdashers' Company 1629–30 and who died in 1631 (his son was also called Robert). A Robert Jeoffries, described as a gentleman of Westminster, was employed during the Commonwealth to keep account of officers and soldiers serving in Ireland (1652), see *Acts and Ordinances of the Interregnum*, ed. by C.H. Firth and R.S. Rait (1911), vol II, pp.608, 714 **16** Nicholl, p.124 **17** GL MS. 16981/1. Apprentices in the Ironmongers' Company were originally bound for ten years from the age of fourteen, reduced to seven years by the seventeenth century. Geffery's indenture of apprenticeship has not survived. This example bound Thomas Cotton apprentice to Richard Peate in 1635. Thomas Cotton senior was MP for St Germans, near Landrake, Cornwall – another link between the Company and Cornwall **18** The Ironmongers' ordinances of 1498 specified surety and bond of £100 for each apprentice, who had to be at least fourteen years old and serve an apprenticeship of ten years. Equivalent modern values derived from E.H. Phelps Brown and Sheila V. Hopkins, 'Seven centuries of the prices of consumables compared with builders' wage rates', *Economica*, November 1956, and the UK Retail Price Index 2012, www.wolfbane.com/rpi **19** CMIC, 3 July 1638, GL MS. 16967/4 **20** Daniel Defoe, *The Complete English Tradesman* (1726) vol I, pp.5–6 **21** CMIC, op. cit., 8 August 1637 **22** The copperplate map-view and the 'Agas' woodcut map of London depicting Ironmongers' Hall are reproduced in *The A to Z of Elizabethan London*, compiled by Adrian Prockter and Robert Taylor, London Topographical Society (1979) **23** CMIC, 18 January 1586, GL MS. 16967/1 **24** Ibid., 27 April 1699, GL MS. 16967/7 **25** Nicholl, pp.434–8 **26** ME/326, 18 May 1669, CRO **27** ME/330, 11 December 1675, CRO **28** Robert Geffery's will, op. cit.

2 | MASTER IRONMONGER

The Mercers, Grocers, Drapers, Fishmongers, Goldsmiths, Skinners,[1] Merchant Taylors, Haberdashers, Salters, Ironmongers, Vintners and Clothworkers are justly proud to be renowned as the 'Great Twelve' livery companies of the City of London, heading a list which continues to increase in number. The roots of these companies lie in the medieval guilds which held a grip on the trade, wealth and politics of the City, and in the seventeenth century membership of a livery company was still essential to an aspiring artisan, tradesman or merchant. Beginning with an apprenticeship, a young man such as Robert Geffery learned his master's skills and assisted him. Towards the end of the seven years' training, Geffery may have assumed some of his elderly master's responsibilities, which would have eased the launch of his career without a large injection of capital. On completion of the apprenticeship, Geffery swore the freeman's oath and was licensed to practice according to the rules and regulations of the Ironmongers' Company.

A conscientious and prosperous freeman normally proceeded to the livery, and Geffery took this step, watched with pride by his former master, Richard Peate, in September 1646.[2] Geffery now faced an increase in his quarterly 'fines' (fees) and it was incumbent on him to purchase sufficient cloth to make a voluminous hooded gown faced with fur – the Ironmongers' livery. The status of liveryman brought responsibilities: liverymen were called upon to serve on the Company's committees, to view and search shops to ensure that trading standards were upheld, to help with the administration of charities, and their attendance was required at church services, dinners and ceremonies. With many years' experience behind him, a liveryman might be elected Junior Warden, then Senior Warden and ultimately Master. Liverymen constituted the mercantile elite of the mid-seventeenth-century City and exercised political influence through a vote in the City's shrieval, mayoral and parliamentary elections. Thus when in 1630 Robert Geffery was apprenticed to Richard Peate, he was on the path that led to his becoming a freeman (1637), liveryman (1646), Master Ironmonger (1667, 1685), Sheriff (1673), Alderman (1676) and Lord Mayor in 1685. His career was all the more remarkable for the events it spanned: Civil War, the execution of King Charles I, plague, fire, war, riots and revolution.

TYRANNY, CIVIL WAR AND THE INTERREGNUM

England was without a Parliament between 1629 and 1640, during which time King Charles I imposed crippling taxes and customs duties upon his subjects. During the 1640s the country was ravaged by Civil War and, following the execution of the King in 1649, England was without a monarch until 1660. For most of Charles's 'eleven years tyranny' (1629–40), Robert Geffery was serving his apprenticeship to Richard Peate and there is no indication that he was riotous or obstreperous, as apprentices tended to be. Having served a dutiful apprenticeship, Geffery was granted the freedom of the Ironmongers' Company in 1637, not an auspicious time for a young man to set up on his own. King Charles had increased customs duties, and ship money (a tax on property to pay for His Majesty's fleet) had been levied on Londoners since 1634. The King's demands for 'forced loans' to subsidise the war with Scotland and his creation of a new corporation of tradesmen and artisans in 1636, dampened enterprise and stirred resentment among merchants of the City livery companies.

PREVIOUS PAGE
Period room at the
Geffrye Museum
representing a typical
parlour in a London
merchant's house, c.1695

ABOVE
Cheapside as Geffery
knew it. An engraving
showing the Cheapside
Cross, conduit and the
procession to welcome
Marie de Medici on a visit
to her daughter, Queen
Henrietta Maria, in 1638

The Civil War of the 1640s saw the capital and the country divided into factions and, with Oliver Cromwell's soldiers patrolling the streets, London was parliamentarian by *force majeur*. Most liverymen of the City companies were royalists by nature, and this applied to the Ironmonger, Thomas Thorold (Master 1634–5, 1644–6) who saw active service in the King's army alongside his fellow Ironmonger, Sir Hugh Windham Bt (Master 1638–9, 1642–3); Sir Christopher Clitherow (Master 1618–9, 1624–5 and Lord Mayor 1635–6) was another royalist. Royalists they might be, but members of the Ironmongers' Company took a stand against the financial demands of King Charles I, resolutely refusing to contribute some £50,000 to support the King's cause (but later compromising). The Company was required to provide armour, pikes and swords from its armoury to help equip the Earl of Essex's parliamentary army in 1642, but drew the line at the storage of fifty barrels of gunpowder at the hall.[3] The Civil War had a detrimental effect on mercantile activity: Ironmongers complained about the deadness of trade and keenly defended their own interests, raising objections to an application by John Browne, the King's gun and cannon-founder, for a monopoly of cast ironware, and as a result the patent was called in (Browne already held the monopoly to make and sell iron ordnance and shot).[4] During the upheaval of national politics and Civil War, trading Ironmongers were chiefly concerned to safeguard their own futures against competition. The younger members were particularly active, petitioning their seniors to take steps to prevent 'the great abuse of forreners [who were not freemen of the City] in bringing their wares of ironworke, nails, locks and other iron ware of severall sorts, to London and the suburbs' for sale.[5]

Ships lay idle in the Thames, markets and shops closed and bankruptcies hit hard during the 1640s. Nevertheless, men such as Izaak Walton, William Turner and Robert Geffery kept a low profile and some merchants managed to make a good living. As John Paige wrote, 'In these dangerous times it's good for men to be circumspect and cautious of what they say', and to continue to trade as best they could – there was money to be made in supplying the army and navy, for instance.[6] The Court of the Ironmongers' Company bewailed 'the distracted and troublesome times',[7] and the 'loans' which forced the Company to sell some of its plate in 1644. Yet in many ways membership of a livery company brought security in times of hardship and instability: members could be confident of mutual support in all aspects of personal and professional life, and poor members and their widows were helped by legacies and charity. Apprentices could be troublemakers *en masse*, but Ironmongers generally, including Robert Geffery, were conservative, Anglican and royalist.

There was one maverick Ironmonger who did cause trouble during the 1640s: Henry Walker, a zealous Puritan and an 'arrant Rascall'.[8] Having served his apprenticeship to Robert Holland, an Ironmonger of Newgate Market, Walker abandoned his trade in gridirons and gads (iron wedges) to indulge in seditious pamphleteering and preaching. Following King Charles I's attempt to arrest five Members of Parliament in January 1642, Walker stirred up agitation and when he chucked one of his pamphlets into His Majesty's coach 'in the very face of the King', he was arrested and imprisoned.[9] Despite his radical youth, Walker remained a member of the Ironmongers' Company and ended his days as a minister of the Church of England in Surrey.[10]

Unlike Henry Walker, Geffery remained aloof from the politics of the 1640s, being more concerned about consolidating his position within the Ironmongers' Company. By the time he was admitted to the livery in 1646, his former master, Richard Peate, was 'one of the ancients of the Company' and by 1649 Peate had fallen on hard times – an indication of the economic difficulties of the 1640s and

The destruction of the Cheapside Cross on the corner of Cheapside with Wood Street, 1643. Built in 1290, it marked a resting place of Queen Eleanor's coffin. The cross was attacked by Puritans because it was a symbol of catholicism. An engraving of 1764

the decline of ironmongery as a trade. Peate could not afford to go abroad during the political turmoil and Civil War of the mid-seventeenth century, as some wealthy merchants did, and he was too old to change his ways. Whereas the younger generation of Ironmongers widened their horizons as merchants and entrepreneurs dealing in various commodities and prospered thereby, Richard Peate being about eighty years old, and Mrs Peate about seventy, could not make ends meet. They were forced to appeal to the Ironmongers' Company for financial support and after Peate's death (c.1653), his widow was grateful for charitable donations from the Company.[11] Richard Peate's son, Richard junior and his grandson William, fared better and maintained the family's connection with the Ironmongers' Company. Geffery had reason to be grateful to Richard Peate, and his will left £150 to be divided between Henry Peate's children, the descendants of Richard.

Any thoughts Robert Geffery might have entertained of returning to Cornwall during this volatile period were dismissed. The south-east of Cornwall, where his roots lay, was particularly dangerous, for here the Earl of Essex spearheaded an attack by the parliamentary forces upon royalist strongholds: Saltash, Plymouth and Launceston became battlegrounds (a strategic factor being the Queen's presence at Pendennis Castle). Essex's campaign in the west met with disaster at Lostwithiel, where his men were surrounded by those loyal to King Charles I (1644). At Geffery's birthplace, Landrake, a Puritan held sway, Jasper Hicks, who berated his congregation from the pulpit of St Michael's Church for some thirty years.

So Geffery saw out the Civil War and Interregnum in London, where life was austere and difficult but not as violent as in south-east Cornwall. The apprentices rioted in 1640 (demonstrating their distaste for Archbishop Laud), and there was opposition to the poll tax of 1641 when the calling out of the Trained Bands (the City militia) created panic. Once the King left the capital early in 1642, the Puritan regime came into force and in May 1643 'the furious and zealous people' demolished 'that stately Crosse in Cheapside' (erected in memory of Queen Eleanor). Effigies of the Pope were set on fire and *The Book of Sports* (1617 and promoted by King Charles I in 1633) was burned by the common hangman, signifying a halt to sports and recreations on Sundays and holidays.[12] As agitation gave way to austerity, theatres were shut and church services on Christmas Day were banned.

LIVERYMAN

Having advanced from freeman to liveryman of the Ironmongers' Company in September 1646, Geffery exercised his right to appear at meetings of the Quarterly Court at Ironmongers' Hall in Fenchurch Street. These Court meetings dealt with the government and internal affairs of the Company such as trade disputes between Ironmongers and other companies, charities, properties and the membership and discipline of members. The Master, Wardens and Court liaised with the Lord Mayor and the City Corporation, and occasionally made representations to the monarch. There was no distinction between the Court and the livery of the Ironmongers' Company at this time – the Master, two Wardens and at least thirteen liverymen constituted a Court.[13] Geffery attended his first Quarterly Court in January 1647 and soon made his presence felt. In November he was among the liverymen who accompanied the Master and Wardens to the Lord Mayor's dinner, the first of many civic dinners that he was to attend. In January of the next year, and again in 1653, Geffery was appointed a 'viewer' to inspect Ironmongers' shops to see that the wares were of good quality and being offered at a fair price, indicating that he was experienced and carried authority in the trade. Geffery impressed his seniors and was soon involved with all the concerns of the Company, serving as an auditor (1658–9, evidently he was a capable accountant), on the committee dealing with the Irish estate, and on the barge committee, which took the prudent decision that for the time being the cost of building a ceremonial barge was prohibitive.[14]

Geffery's diligent participation in the Company's affairs brought him contacts among the liverymen of the other 'Great Twelve' companies, who were his companions at the City's social events, church services and important state occasions such as the celebrations on Ash Wednesday 1654. The Lord Mayor issued orders for liverymen to attend the Lord Protector, to wear their gowns and hoods, to be in place by 10 o'clock and to remain there until 'His Highnesse, the

Lord Protector, and his Councill be passed by'. Geffery was there, standing to attention in front of his Company's unfurled banners and streamers,[15] to witness Lord Protector Oliver Cromwell process through the City with all the pomp of a monarch. This ostentatious display on the day that marked the start of Lent and a period of abstinence did not meet with the approval of royalists such as Geffery and John Evelyn (1620–1706), whose diary recorded his distaste at the sight of Cromwell, 'in contradiction to all custome and decency', feasting at the Lord Mayor's table and riding in triumph through the City.[16]

MARRIAGE

The decade of 1650 to 1660 was one of entrenchment for Geffery. He married a Mercer's daughter and settled in Lime Street; he invested in the East India Company and the Levant Company and established his reputation as a man of integrity, a worthy citizen, a churchgoer and an active liveryman of the Ironmongers' Company. Liverymen of the 'Great Twelve' companies mingled at City functions and this was probably how Geffery came across Luke Cropley, a liveryman of the premier company of the 'Great Twelve', whose sons were also Mercers. This was the entrée to Geffery's marriage to Priscilla (sometimes spelled Percilla), the eldest daughter of Luke and Judith Cropley, at the Mercers' Chapel, Mercers' Hall, Cheapside, on 9 September 1651,[17] one of the lucky days for a wedding, so it was said. Robert was thirty-eight, his bride Priscilla was eighteen years old. Robert's age at the time of his marriage reflected the slow start of his career in the difficult circumstances of the 1640s, but the 1650s, which saw him married and settled in a mansion in Lime Street, augured well: marriage to the daughter of a Mercer who was an attorney and landowner, cemented Geffery's mercantile and social credibility. His association with the Cropleys presented financial and social opportunities and was a turning point in his life.

Geffery's father-in-law, Luke Cropley, was a well-connected attorney who owned a farm in County Durham, a property in the City of London, a family house in Clerkenwell and he held the lease of a house and land in Stepney from the Mercers' Company.[18] As an attorney practising in the common courts (in effect a solicitor), Luke Cropley earned a good income, and on Robert Geffery's marriage to his daughter, he presented the couple with £800 (some £105,000 at 2012 values), an advance on Priscilla's inheritance.[19] Cropley evidently approved of his son-in-law, to whom he left £50 and the executorship of his will following his death in 1662, attributed to a fever (he was buried at St James's, Clerkenwell).[20]

The marriage of Robert and Priscilla at the Mercers' Chapel, 'a fair and beautiful chapel arched over with stone', was the choice of the bride and her

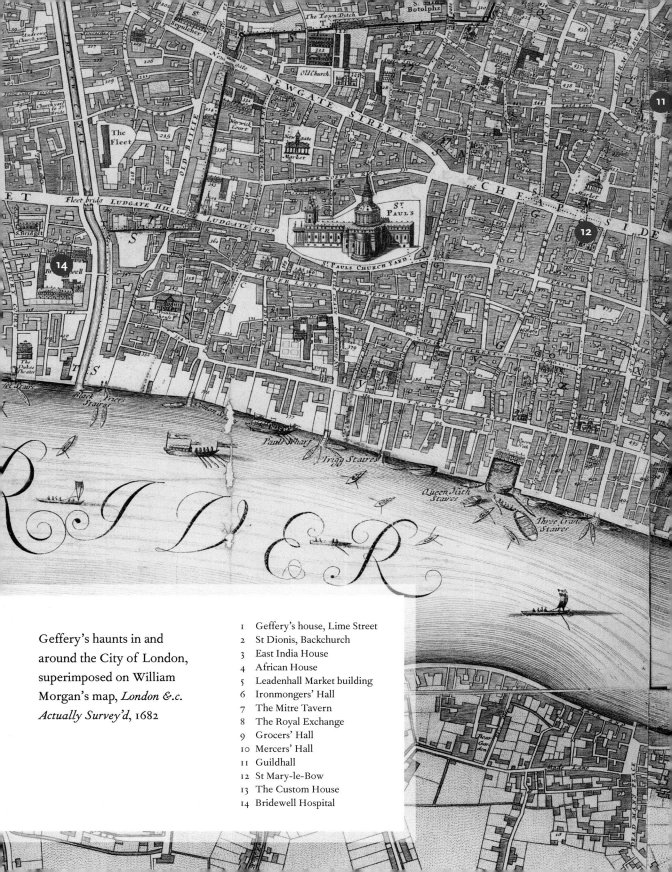

Geffery's haunts in and around the City of London, superimposed on William Morgan's map, *London &c. Actually Survey'd*, 1682

1   Geffery's house, Lime Street
2   St Dionis, Backchurch
3   East India House
4   African House
5   Leadenhall Market building
6   Ironmongers' Hall
7   The Mitre Tavern
8   The Royal Exchange
9   Grocers' Hall
10 Mercers' Hall
11 Guildhall
12 St Mary-le-Bow
13 The Custom House
14 Bridewell Hospital

family.[21] Flowers, herbs and rushes were strewn in front of Priscilla on her way into the chapel, where the ceremony was conducted by Dr Thomas Horton, Divinity Professor of Gresham College and Rector of St Mary, Colechurch (the Mercers' Company was the patron of St Mary, Colechurch, which was situated close to Mercers' Hall).[22] Guests at the wedding bore branches of rosemary and when the couple emerged from the service, wheat was scattered on Priscilla's head. This was the last time the bride would wear her hair down as a maiden, thereafter she would wind her hair up in a modest fashion, as befitted a married woman. Her family hosted the wedding feast, probably at Mercers' Hall, when the traditional bride-cake and sops in wine were passed round in a hallowed 'knitting cup'. There was music, drinking and jesting, culminating in putting the bridegroom to bed.

Robert and Priscilla Geffery's wedding celebration reflected the optimistic mood of London following the battle of Worcester on 3 September. King Charles II had fled, war was at an end and Oliver Cromwell entered London in triumph on 12 September, all of which promised well for the trade, economy and stability of the City. Personally, Geffery was gratified by his liaison with the Cropley family, and it was with some pride that he incorporated the Cropley arms into his own. When he was granted a knighthood in 1673 he was quick to register his coat of arms officially with the College of Arms, whereupon the Cropley reference was dropped (see pages 92, 94, 96).[23]

LIME STREET

Once married, Gefffery put down roots in Lime Street, which wound between Fenchurch Street and Leadenhall Street in the City. The area had once been an affluent residential neighbourhood of Roman Londinium, close to the forum and basilica and the site of opulent third and fourth-century houses decorated with mosaics and warmed by under-floor heating. The name 'Limstrate' was first recorded in the 1170s and 1180s, denoting a place where lime burners and sellers congregated; they were superseded by potters and bell-makers, and by the fifteenth century merchants occupied 'divers fair houses' in the street (Lime Street is now dominated by Lloyds of London at its northern end).[24] When Robert and Priscilla Geffery lived in Lime Street, the topography of the area was defined by the fifteenth-century Leadenhall Market building and the adjacent market places. The parish church was the traditional focal point of a community but there was no church in Lime Street Ward (it covered such a small area it was commonly called Farthing Ward). Thus the fortress-like Leadenhall formed both a historic landmark and the centre of activity, bounded on the north by a major

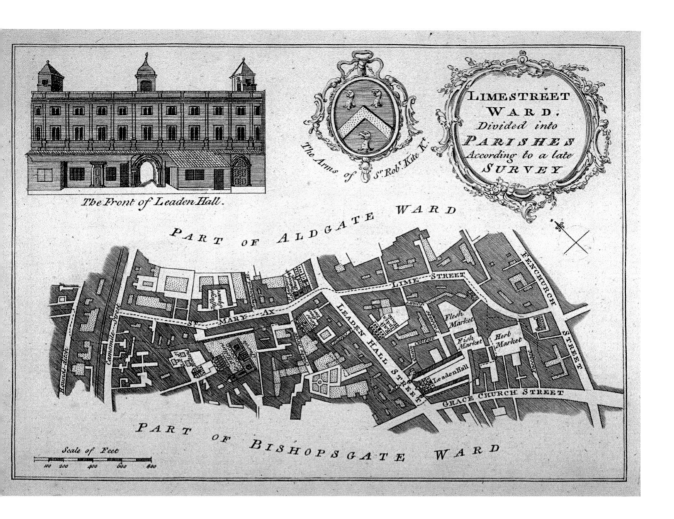

The Front of Leaden Hall.

The Arms of Sr. Robt. Kite Kt.

LIMESTREET WARD, Divided into PARISHES According to a late SURVEY

PART OF ALDGATE WARD

PART OF BISHOPSGATE WARD

Scale of Feet

Lime Street Ward with a vignette of Leadenhall Market, engraved by Thomas Bowen, 1771. Geffery was Deputy of the Ward 1662–7 and 1668–76

thoroughfare, Leadenhall Street, and on the east by Lime Street, from where alleys and passages led to a cluster of fish, flesh and herb markets. Another local landmark, well-known to City merchants, was the mansion in Leadenhall Street belonging to Sir Christopher Clitherow, Governor of the East India Company from 1638–41. The house served as the Company's headquarters until the move to the neighbouring Craven House in 1648. From there the East India Company extended its hold on the area, acquiring land on the west side of Lime Street as far south as Geffery's house, by leasing and building warehouses and eventually occupying the palatial East India House in 1729.

'The Newest & Exactest Mapp of the most Famous Cities London and Westminster, with their Suburbs; and the manner of their Streets', by Thomas Porter (1654) depicts a three-gabled house on the west side of Lime Street which may well represent Geffery's mansion. It was a short walk from there to several of his haunts – Ironmongers' Hall, East India House, the Royal Exchange, African

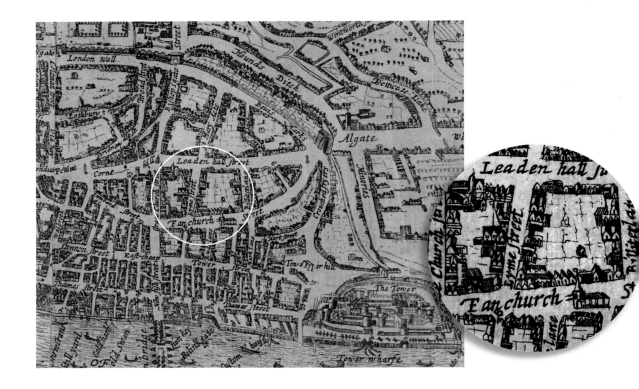

House, St Dionis, Backchurch, and Leadenhall Market (see pages 40–1). Significantly for Geffery, in 1622 the City had authorised a market for the sale of iron and cutlery brought to London from the provinces to be held in the Green Yard at Leadenhall. This centred on the Nail Gallery, a substantial two storey building with a garret, where nails, knives, cutlery, locks, hinges and other wares made of iron were sold. There were other shops and warehouses at Leadenhall where leather, wood and cloth were stored, also a calico warehouse used by the East India Company, in addition to the stalls selling fresh provisions.[25] The proximity of Geffery's house to Leadenhall Market and the fact that in 1673 he leased a plot on the north-east side of the market to build an 'open hall', and in 1700 leased another two properties facing the piazza,[26] confirms that he had interests there, while his mansion, nearby in Lime Street, with its counting-house and parlour, provided the base for business transactions, banking and entertaining. Here Geffery kept his accounts, correspondence and ready money; when he sold his land in Cornwall to Sir Richard Edgcumbe, he insisted that the deposit was delivered to his dwelling house in Lime Street.[27] The multi-purpose house also accommodated apprentices and servants, while garrets and vaults provided storage for merchandise.[28]

OPPOSITE
Thomas Porter's map of
London, Westminster and
the suburbs, 1654. A detail
shows 'Lyme Street' and
a house on the west side
of the street that could be
where Geffery lived

BELOW
Detail from Ogilby
and Morgan's map of
1676, showing Geffery's
properties on the west
side of Lime Street. The
wavy line depicts the
extent of the Great Fire
in September 1666. The
dotted line is the Ward
boundary

Geffery first paid a year's rent (£25) for his Lime Street mansion at Easter 1652 and he was still living there at the time of his death in 1704. The property had been bequeathed to the Rector of St Dionis, Backchurch, by Giles de Kelseye in 1377, on condition that a lamp was kept burning day and night, to his memory, in front of the high altar.[29] De Kelseye's house, tenements and appurtenances then passed through many hands, Roger Vivian being the lease-holder immediately before Geffery.[30] Robert and Priscilla Geffery lived in the house for some fourteen years before it was destroyed by the Great Fire of London in September 1666. Once rebuilt, the dwelling house was one of the two largest private houses in Lime Street, with sixteen hearths (most had six).[31] The mansion, approached through a gate and courtyard, was now well-suited to someone with political and commercial ambitions. There was as yet no official Mansion House for the use of the Lord Mayor during his year in office. Grocers' Hall, rebuilt at the expense of Sir John Moore in 1682, was used for mayoral banquets, as it was for Geffery's inaugural dinner in 1685, but otherwise as Sheriff and later as Lord Mayor, Geffery entertained at home (see pages 95, 118). Plate, household goods and jewels valued at £408 were found at his house after his death, when his horses and 'chariot' were sold for £54, indicating that even in old age, Geffery lived comfortably, with his niece as companion/housekeeper, three resident servants and a coachman in charge of the stables.[32]

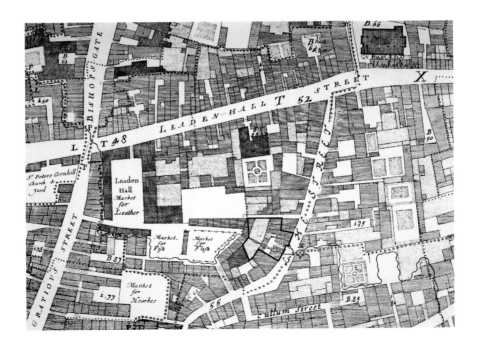

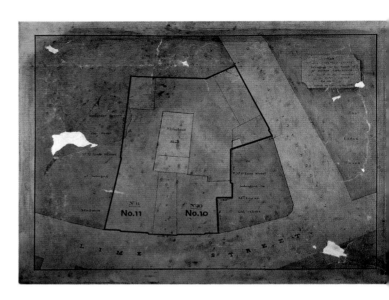

NEIGHBOURS

When the Gefferys lived in Lime Street it was inhabited by merchants and men of repute and wealth, such as Francis Tryon, a usurer and jeweller who was gagged and robbed of £1,050 in money and £4,000 worth of jewels at his Lime Street house in 1664. The money and jewels were found in the possession of 'Colonel' James Turner, 'a mad, swearing, confident fellow', according to the diarist Samuel Pepys (1633–1703).[33] Turner was promptly hanged at the northern end of Lime Street – a gruesome sight that attracted a large number of onlookers.

Sir James Cambell (Master of the Ironmongers' Company three times and Lord Mayor 1629–30) was a former Alderman of Lime Street Ward, and his brother-in-law, another Ironmonger, Sir Christopher Clitherow, lived in Leadenhall Street, around the corner from Lime Street, until his death in 1641. Sir Charles Thorold, Master of the Ironmongers' Company at the time of Geffery's death and his successor as Alderman of Cordwainer Ward, lived nearby, and William Warren, co-owner of a ship with Geffery, was another neighbour. Mathew Gibbon, a draper, was a resident of Lime Street Ward, and his young relative, Edward (1666–1736, grandfather of the historian), attended Geffery's church, St Dionis.

Whilst living in Lime Street, Geffery witnessed the inauguration of the Penny Post by his neighbour, William Dockwra (1635–1716). Dockwra had a varied career, at the Custom House, as an inventor, the founder of the Penny Post in

ABOVE LEFT
James Turner, convicted of robbing Francis Tryon of Lime Street, was hanged at the corner of Lime Street with Leadenhall Street, 1664

ABOVE RIGHT
A plan of the site of Robert Geffery's house in Lime Street. The freehold of the property belonged to the parish of St Dionis, Backchurch. Surveyed in 1847 by Richard Suter, dated 1853

1680 and as Master of the Armourers' Company (1692–4). He was also a ship-owner trading along the Guinea Coast of Africa, so he may have met Geffery in this context or at the Custom House, before they became neighbours. Dockwra's house in Lime Street became the hub of the Penny Post, the 'Principal Office to which all Accompts etc. are daily transacted...an ingenious undertaking...so extraordinarily useful in the facilitating of commerce and mutual correspondence',[34] and a facility which Geffery surely appreciated. The house had previously been occupied by Sir Robert Abdy and with its great hall, parlours and five bedchambers it accommodated Dockwra's Penny Post Office and his family of nine children. Letters received here were marked 'Penny Post Paid', with the initial L at the centre, indicating Lime Street, a mark considered by some philatelists to be the world's first postage stamp. Dockwra's endeavours were thwarted by the arrest of his partner, Robert Murray, and opposition from the Duke of York; consequently the headquarters of the Penny Post moved to Crosby Hall and Dockwra lost his business.

The 1720 edition of Strype's *Survey of the Cities of London and Westminster* confirms that Lime Street was, at that date, still 'a Place well inhabited by Merchants and others of Repute'. Pewterers' Hall, with its paved courtyard and bowling alley, stood on the south-west side of the street and 'Near unto this Hall is the passage to Leadenhall Market; a little more South is a good House, formerly the Seat of Sir Robert Jeffreys, Knt and Alderman'.[35] The location of Geffery's 'Seat' can be further defined because the freehold of the property was owned by the parish of St Dionis, shown on a survey of 1847 and plans of 1884 as numbers nine, ten and eleven Lime Street, with a total frontage of 61 feet 3 inches facing the street. A gateway and passage led from the street to the court-yard (later covered) and the main entrance of the house.[36] Geffery's objections to a new building 'in the passage to Leadenhall Market...on the north side of the Green Yard' because it obscured his light, points to his property being on the south side of the passage that led from Lime Street to the Green Yard and Leadenhall Market.[37]

GEFFERY'S PROPERTIES

Two years after his marriage, Geffery consolidated his base in Lime Street by leasing a neighbouring apothecary's house and, in June 1666, he leased a third house in the street (see page 58). After the destruction wrought by the Great Fire of London later that year, he applied for permission to lay the foundations of properties in Lime Street, Blackfriars Lane and Thames Street (the buildings in Duke Humphreys near Blackfriars Lane, and in Thames Street were most

probably warehouses).[38] His property-holdings were to be extended by the lease of a warehouse in Crutched Friars from the Ironmongers' Company after the Great Fire had destroyed those he owned in Thames Street, and the acquisition of a building plot at Leadenhall Market (1673), where, in 1700, he leased two more dwellings backing onto his own house. Further afield, he purchased land at Rame, Milbrook and Maker on a peninsula south of Landrake in Cornwall (1669), selling a portion of it to Sir Richard Edgcumbe of Mount Edgcumbe in 1675. He obtained a grant of land in Ireland in 1667: 192 acres in Carragheen in the south-east (which gave its name to Carrageen, Irish moss, a seaweed) and 67 acres in Garrymoreish, County Tipperary.[39] Geffery's Irish interests stemmed from the Ironmongers' estate, the Manor of Lizard, Londonderry, which he visited with the Company's agent, Paul Canning, in 1658.[40] The Irish colony, or 'Plantation' as it was called, had been King James I's initiative for the development of Ulster by the City livery companies. The 'Great Twelve' companies invested substantial resources in the development and settlement of their Irish estates. The inhospitable terrain, the poverty of the inhabitants and the devastation wrought by the rebellion and 'great massacre' of 1641, followed by the ravages of the parliamentarian troops in 1650 presented a formidable challenge. As a Governor (1670–1), auditor (1673–5) and an Assistant of the Irish Society in 1683, Geffery was at the administrative core of the City's programme for the colonisation of Ulster.

Men of Geffery's standing were inclined to purchase a country house as a retreat from the crowded City during hot summers and a haven during outbreaks of the plague. Not so Geffery; his base was in the City of London and only in old age did he escape to lodgings in Surrey during the summer. His personal and commercial interests lay in the City, where his properties could be let when not required – tenants owed him some £80 in 1704 and, in addition, his executors received £3,621 10 shillings (about £525,000 at 2012 values) from Mr John Harris 'for several properties'.[41] Renowned as a judicious magistrate and an experienced auditor, Geffery was also a sharp-witted property-holder, whose advice was valued by his contemporaries. He was consulted by his cousin, Ann Lower, over the sale of Trelaske to a merchant named John Addis in 1703,[42] and Alderman Thomas Lewis sought Geffery's approbation of his family's property transactions and trusts.[43]

A GOOD AND HONEST CITIZEN

Geffery's roots in Lime Street were strengthened by his election as Deputy of the Ward in 1662. He served for five years and for a second term from 1668 until 1676, when he was elected Alderman of Cordwainer Ward. The twenty-six Wards of the City constituted the basis for local government and they were essential units for policing, taxation, justice, the militia and politics. The inhabitants of Lime Street Ward chose good and honest men for positions of responsibility: a Beadle, two scavengers, sixteen inquest men, four constables and four Common Councillors, one of whom was the Alderman representing the Ward on the Court of Aldermen, which had the Lord Mayor at its head. Geffery's first duty for Lime Street Ward was as a scavenger, responsible for vaults, sewers and drains and for collecting the levy on these amenities. The following year, 1655, he was one of the constables for the Ward; in 1656 he acted as the scribe (recording official business), and in December 1659 he was elected a Common Councillor and foreman of the Wardmote inquest (the local court), taking up his duties in 1660.[44] While Deputy of the Ward, Geffery was consulted by the East India Company in the hope that the tax assessment on East India House might be reduced. Quite rightly, Deputy Geffery decreed that the assessment was fair and could not be altered.[45] His thirteen years' experience as Deputy of Lime Street Ward was the pupilage for the twenty-five years he served as Alderman of Cordwainer Ward, a larger Ward bordering on Cheapside.

OPPOSITE
The Alderman of Lime Street Ward *(right)* and his Deputy, illustrated in the manuscript *A Caveatt for the Citty of London* by Hugh Alley, 1598. Geffery served as Deputy of the Ward 1662–7 and 1668–76

'A merry man'

Robert Geffery was among the group of merry men who met the diarist Samuel Pepys at the Thames waterside on 22 March 1662. Geffery's fellow Ironmonger, Sir John Lewis Bt, was there (he traded in silk through the East India Company), along with Alderman Thomas Lewis (who supplied victuals to the naval ships) 'and several other great merchants',[46] for a meeting with Pepys, who was Clerk to the Navy Board and responsible for building and repairing ships and supplying stores, victuals and equipment to His Majesty's fleet. Pepys was accompanied by Sir William Penn, Commissioner of the Navy, and the purpose of the meeting was to inspect the *Lewis*, a thirty-two-gun merchant ship owned by the Lewises, later used as a ship-of-war.

Pepys had contracts at his fingertips, especially regarding supplies and equipment for the navy. At the time of this meeting with Geffery in the spring of 1662, the supply of anchors, chains and ironmongery to the navy (especially important during the Dutch wars) lay with many small contractors. Geffery may have had a foot in that door, or been hoping to place one, and it is likely that his friends Alderman Lewis and Sir John Lewis provided the introduction to Pepys. Whatever the reason for Geffery's presence, the meeting proved jovial. Pepys enjoyed Geffery's company, referring to him as 'one Jefferys, a merry man that is a fumbler; and he and I called brothers, and he made all the mirth in the company. We had a very fine dinner, and all our wifes' healths with seven or nine guns [flagons] apiece. And exceeding merry we were, and so home by barge again... and so to supper and to bed – having drank a great deal of wine'.[47] Pepys described Geffery as a 'fumbler', that is to say 'an unperforming husband, one that is insufficient, a weak Brother'.[48] As his diary reveals, Pepys pursued an active sex life, yet he did not 'lie with his wife' for months on end and both he and Geffery were childless – fumblers and brothers.

Church and Faith

From the day of his baptism at St Michael's Church, Landrake, on 24 May 1613, to his burial at St Dionis, Backchurch, on 10 March 1704, Geffery was an unwavering member of the Church of England. As a child he would have been taught to read the Bible and taken to services at the church where he had been baptised; as a young man in London he lived through the strict Puritan era and heard the rantings of preachers. With the Restoration of the monarchy in 1660 came the enforcement of the Book of Common Prayer, and with the reign of King James II came the Jesuits and the opening of 'mass-houses'. The revolution of 1688–9 brought the Dutch Prince William and his Protestant wife, Mary, to the throne, succeeded in 1702 by the pious Anglican Queen Anne. Geffery's lifetime spanned six reigns and an Interregnum, throughout which he maintained his steady faith and devotion to the Church of England and the Book of Common Prayer.

Certainly from 1652 and possibly since his marriage the previous year, Geffery attended St Dionis, Backchurch, on the corner of Lime Street and Fenchurch Street and in Langbourn Ward. The parish included the southern half of Lime Street, the northern part of the street being in the parish of St Andrew, Undershaft. The name St Dionis derived from St Denys, patron saint of France, and Backchurch denoted the church's situation, set back from the street, or possibly the 'Bac' referred to Godwin Bac, a monk of Canterbury. The medieval church had been repaired and extended in 1632 under the supervision of John Warner, Chaplain to King Charles I. Warner was replaced by Nathaniel Hardy in 1643, a Presbyterian who recanted and became the favourite preacher of Anglican civic leaders and royalists such as Geffery. Hardy accompanied the deputation to The Hague to welcome the exiled King Charles II in 1660 and was subsequently appointed the King's Chaplain. During the course of the fifty years that Geffery worshipped at St Dionis, Hardy was succeeded by Reverend George May and from 1680 by Reverend Lionel Gatford, who was to conduct

The diarist Samuel Pepys, painted by John Hayls, 1666. Pepys commissioned this portrait and was confident that it would be 'a very fine picture. He [Hayls] promises it shall be as good as my wife's, and I sit to have it full of shadows and so break my neck looking over my shoulder to make the posture for him to work by'

St Dionis, Backchurch, rebuilt to designs by Sir Christopher Wren (1670–4). An engraving by George Shepherd, 1813. Geffery contributed to the cost of rebuilding and donated luxurious furnishings. As a Churchwarden (1670–1) and member of the vestry, he urged Wren and the surveyors to proceed with the rebuilding. Geffery and his wife Priscilla were buried in the church, which was demolished in 1878

Geffery's funeral service in 1704.

Geffery first participated in a meeting of the parish vestry of St Dionis in December 1652, which suggests that he was already familiar with the church. He contributed £3 (towards a total cost of £307) for the renovation of the building in 1654;[49] he served as an auditor of the accounts and in 1667 he was nominated to a committee to oversee the fate of the poor children of the parish. Having no children of his own, Geffery's compassion was channelled towards the City's orphans, the poor children of Landrake, and in his London parish he was concerned with the welfare of babes and infants who were sometimes abandoned on doorsteps or at the church. The problem of 'disposing' of the poor parish children called for a committee, which was led by Geffery and, with a subsidy from parish funds, homes and families were found to care for the children for a specified number of years.[50]

Geffery worshipped at St Dionis for half a century, serving as Churchwarden for the year 1670–1, and both he and his wife were to be buried and commemorated in the church. When he was elected 'Accountant Churchwarden' (the senior Churchwarden) in 1670, Geffery begged to be excused but 'the vestry were unwilling to consent thereto and used many arguments to persuade him to hold office'. He did not seek to evade responsibility but, mindful of his duties as Deputy Alderman and his burgeoning business activities, he was a reluctant Churchwarden. A compromise was reached whereby he served for one year, not two (paying a 40 shilling fine to be excused for the second year).[51] In addition to being a loyal parishioner for several decades and senior Churchwarden for a year, Geffery's mansion and two smaller premises in Lime Street were leased from St Dionis (see pages 45, 47, 58).

At vestry meetings Geffery came across Daniel Rawlinson, landlord of one of the City's busiest taverns, The Mitre, in Fenchurch Street. Rawlinson was a prosperous and popular local figure, for he was also the proprietor of The Crown and Three Sugar Loaves in Fenchurch Street, where the fashionable new drink, tea, was sold. John Battersby, an apothecary at the sign of The Great Helmet in Fenchurch Street, was also active in parish affairs (Rawlinson and Battersby were both friends of Samuel Pepys). Sir Henry Tulse (who later moved to St Margaret, Lothbury), Peter Hoet, Philip Jackson, Michael Markland the apothecary, Francis Tryon and Thomas Turgis were others who attended vestry meetings with Geffery. As Deputy of Lime Street Ward, a Churchwarden and a tenant of the parish, Geffery often took the lead at these meetings, organising parish affairs such as the maintenance and later the rebuilding of the church, the distribution of charity, and at the age of eighty-nine he was still signing warrants to maintain parish children at the workhouse.[52]

Samuel Pepys attended a Sunday service at St Dionis in September 1660, meeting Daniel Rawlinson there.[53] Pepys was impressed by the sermon and he returned to the church four years later on Christmas Day. This time his attention was captured by the women in the congregation, 'and very great store of fine women there is in this church, more than I know anywhere else', he commented appreciatively, (Geffery's wife, Priscilla, would have been among the 'very great store of fine women').[54] In 1666 the Great Fire destroyed St Dionis and, in the chaos that followed, Geffery and other parishioners ensured that the church bell was rescued and that a wall was built around the churchyard to prevent looting. With Battersby and the Churchwardens, Geffery travelled to Romford in Essex in 1667 (where the parish owned land) to organise the sale of the woods there, presumably for felling and use as building material which was in great demand.[55] The rebuilding of the church coincided with Geffery's term as senior Churchwarden and because the project was close to his heart, he pursued it energetically. Workmen were recruited for a fortnight in December 1670 to clear the debris and, over the next few months, Geffery and the vestry of St Dionis conferred with Sir Christopher Wren, visiting him at his lodgings in Whitehall, entertaining him at The Mitre Tavern and liaising with the surveyors, Robert Hooke (with whom Geffery dealt on other issues, see pages 61–2), John Oliver and Edward Woodroffe. Geffery kept up the pressure on the surveyors and builders, urging the team 'to promote what in them lyeth, the finishing of the church', especially the covering of the roof before winter set in.[56] These tactics proved successful and St Dionis was one of the first of Wren's fifty-four City churches to be built, although in 1683 Geffery and the vestry were still pestering the architect to complete the steeple and lantern to top the tower.[57]

The rebuilding of St Dionis to designs by Wren (1670–4) was subsidised by wealthy parishioners. Geffery had erected a monument in the church in 1659 (to a dead relative, perhaps his child?),[58] and he was among seven local patrons who gave £100 each towards the total cost of Wren's building (£5,737). Geffery also contributed to the cost of new bells, pews, a clock and dial, and he donated some luxurious furnishings: a velvet carpet with a silk and gold fringe for the communion table, a Book of Common Prayer covered in the same velvet, and a velvet pulpit cushion trimmed with silk and gold tassels. In 1677, soon after the death of his wife, Priscilla, he was granted permission to set up 'trophies' in the church.[59] Members of Priscilla's family had attended St Dionis with her and her husband, and one of her relatives, Thomas Turgis, paid for the new gallery at the west end. Priscilla's niece and namesake, Priscilla Turgis, their relations and Sir Henry Tulse (who had been apprenticed to Thomas Turgis senior and married into the family) were buried at St Dionis, as were Geffery's Cornish relative, John Roberts, and Geffery's servant, Jane Knight. In 1704 Sir Robert Geffery was buried there too, joining his wife, their relatives, friends and maid. His last will and testament left £50 towards the church's debts and made provision for divine service to be celebrated twice every weekday forever (see page 174). Geffery's generosity was recorded on 'a table of benefactors' in the church,[60] upon which his name was inscribed under those of Sir Henry Tulse, (who donated the font, steps and pavement), Philip Jackson (the altarpiece; his wife gave cloths for the communion table), Daniel Rawlinson (brass candelabra) and Sir Arthur Ingram (the communion table and rails). In accordance with Geffery's will, a monument to himself and his wife was commissioned for the church and was in place by 1707 (see below). It was given a conspicuous position on the chancel wall with Geffery's 'ensigns of honour' – a helmet, sword, gauntlets and banners, and his coat of arms emblazoned with jewels (pearls, diamond, topaz), 'he being so ancient and eminent a Magistrate'.[61]

The future of Geffery's parish church came under review in the Victorian era, when the architect G.E. Street proposed a Gothic remodelling of Wren's church. The outcome was even more radical: the church was demolished, a victim of the Union of City Benefices Act (1878). The remains of Sir Robert and Lady Geffery were then re-interred in a tomb at the burial ground alongside the almshouses he had endowed at Shoreditch, now the Geffrye Museum (see page 180). The fittings from St Dionis, including the marble font, the pulpit, woodwork and plate, went to the new church of St Dionis, Parsons Green, in west London, and some monuments found a home at All Hallows, Lombard Street (demolished in 1939). Fortunately, Sir Robert Geffery's marble monument was saved: it was moved and moved again before it found its present home in the chapel of the Geffrye Museum (see pages 171–3, 183).

THE PLAGUE

Geffery, his wife and household remained in Lime Street throughout the Great Plague of 1665. Others fled: the King and his Court departed to Oxford, Parliament was prorogued and those with estates or relatives in the country deserted London, which came to a standstill. There were few physicians to be found in the capital to care for plague victims, and grass grew in Leadenhall Street and at the Royal Exchange, which was shut for nearly two months, curtailing Geffery's trading activities. Shops, taverns, coffee-houses and some churches closed and infected houses were boarded up, imprisoning the occupants for forty days. Geffery's neighbourhood was not as heavily populated as some City parishes and was inhabited by affluent merchants, which probably accounted for the comparatively low number of deaths from the plague in the parish during the summer of 1665 (twenty-seven, whereas there were 112 victims in the parish of All Hallows, Staining, where Ironmongers' Hall was situated).[62] The first reported incidence in Fenchurch Street, which crossed the south end of Lime Street, occurred in early June and within a few weeks Dr Alexander Burnet, Pepys's physician, who lived there, was dead. Geffery's fellow churchgoer, Daniel Rawlinson, barred the doors of The Mitre Tavern, the favourite hostelry

43

LONNDN 39   From the 12. of Septemb. to the 19. of the same 1665.

Parish	Buried	Plag.	Parish	Buried	Plag.	Parish	Buried	Plag.	Parish	Buried	Plag.
St Alban Woodstreet	23	19	St Clement Eastcheap	5	5	St Margaret Newfishst.	17	13	St Michael Crookedla.	10	10
Alhallows Bark.	41	32	St Dionis Backchurch	10	5	St Margaret Pattons	5	5	St Michael Queenhith	11	6
Alhallows Breadstreet	4	3	St Dunstans East	20	10	St Mary Abchurch	13	9	St Michael Quern	4	2
Alhallows Great	59	53	St Edmund Lumbardst.	4	4	St Mary Aldermanbury	20	16	St Michael Royal	20	17
Ahallows Honilane	1	1	St Ethelborough	16	6	St Mary Aldermary	11	10	St Michael Woodstreet	6	2
Ahallows Less	29	26	St Faiths	6	6	St Mary le Bow	4	2	St Mildred Breadstreet	6	3
Alhallows Lumbardstr	8	7	St Gabriel Fenchurch	5	3	St Mary Bothaw	4	4	St Mildred Poultrey	4	3
Alhallows Staining	16	13	St George Botolphlane			St Mary Colechurch	4	8	St Nicholas Acons	8	5
Alhallows the Wall	41	30	St Gregories by St. Paul	32	23	St Mary Hill	12	8	St Nicholas Coleabby	14	13
St Alphage	25	13	St Hellen	8	5	St Mary Mag. Milkstr.	5	5	St Nicholas Olaves	12	9
St Andrew Hubbard	6	5	St James Dukes place	29	26	St Mary Mag.Oldfishst	16	11	St Olave Hartstreet	20	18
St Andrew Undershaft	25	22	St James Garlickhithe	13	11	St Mary Mounthaw	9	9	St Olave Jewry	7	5
St Andrew Wardrobe	63	54	St John Baptist	7	6	St Mary Summerset	36	34	St Olave Silverstreet	23	17
St Anne Aldersgate	33	28	St John Evangelist			St Mary Stainings	2	2	St Pancras Soperlane	2	2
St Anne Blackfryers	79		St John Zachary	3	2	St Mary Woolchurch	2		St Peter Cheap	4	3
St Antholins Parish	3	3	St Katharine Coleman	44	36	St Mary Woolnoth	9	6	St Peter Cornhil	10	6
St Austins Parish	2	2	St Katharine Creechur.	35	31	St Martins Iremongerl,	2	2	St Peter Paulswharf	12	12
St Barthol.Exchange	5	3	St Lawrence Jewry	5		St Martins Ludgate	21	11	St Peter Poor	12	6
St Bennet Fynck	1		St Lawrence Pountney	22	17	St Martins Orgars	9	7	St Steven Colemanstr.	47	40
St Bennet Gracechurch	5	4	St Leonard Eastcheap			St Martins Outwich	3		St Steven Walbrook.	5	
St Bennet Paulswharf	35	15	St Leonard Fosterlane	34	32	St Martins Vintrey	64	61	St Swithin	19	17
St Bennet Sherehog			St Magnus Parish	9	6	St Matthew Frydaystr.	5	3	St Thomas Apostle	19	13
StBotolph Billingsgate	4	4	St Margaret Lothbury	8	8	St Michael Bassishaw	5	1	Trinity Parish	13	13
Christ Church	55	48	St Margaret Moses	5	5	St Michael Cornhil	14	11	St Vedast alias Fosters	10	9
St Christophers	6	5									

Christned in 97 the Parishes within the Walls — 40   Buried — 1493   Plague — 1189

Parish	Buried	Plag.	Parish	Buried	Plag.	Parish	Buried	Plag.	Parish	Buried	Plag.
St Andrew Holborn	271	247	St Botolph Aldersgate	68	62	St George Southwark	195	176	St Sepulchres Parish	301	214
St Bartholomew Great	21	17	St Botolph Aldgate	623	589	St Giles Cripplegate	456	373	St Thomas Southwark	57	52
St Bartholomew Less	14	12	St Botolph Bishopgate	294	256	St Olave Southwark	530	363	Trinity Minories	12	10
St Bridges	236	180	St Dunstan West	88	79	St Saviour Southwark	427	405	At the Pesthouse	6	6
Bridewel Precinct	52	31									

Christned in the 16 Parishes without the walls — 65   Buried — 3631   Plague — 3070

Parish	Buried	Plag.	Parish	Buried	Plag.	Parish	Buried	Plag.	Parish	Buried	Plag.
Christs Church			St Kath.near the Tower	93	66	St Mary Islington	68	66	St Paul Shadwel		
St John at Hackney	22	18	Lambeth Parish	48	43	St Mary Newington	155	152	Rotherhith Parish	17	13
St Giles in the Fields	149	125	St Leonard Shoreditch	183	173	St Mary Whitechappel	532	502	Stepney Parish	716	686
St James Clerkenwel	77	67	St Magdalen Bermond.	207	180						

Christned in the 12 Out-Parishes in Middlesex and Surrey — 42   Buried — 2258   Plague — 2091

Parish	Buried	Plag.	Parish	Buried	Plag.	Parish	Buried	Plag.
St Clement Danes	163	140	St Martins in the fields	286	225	St Mary Savoy	20	19
St Paul Covent Garden	30	29				St Margaret Westminst.	411	399
						whereof at the Pesthouse		7

Christned in the 5 Parishes in the City and Liberties of Westminster — 29   Buried — 915   Plague — 815

The Diseases and Casualties this Week.

Abortive	5		Kingsevill	2
Aged	43		Lethargy	1
Ague	2		Palsy	1
Appoplexie	1		Plague	7165
Bleeding	2		Rickets	17
Burnt in his Bed by a Candle at St. Giles Cripplegate	1		Rising of the Lights	11
Canker	1		Scowring	5
Childbed	42		Scurvy	2
Chrisomes	18		Spleene	1
Consumption	134		Spotted Feaver	101
Convulsion	64		Stilborne	17
Cough	2		Stone	2
Dropsy	33		Stop. in the Stomak	9
Feaver	309		Strangury	1
Flox and smal Pox	5		Suddenly	1
Frighted	3		Surfeit	49
Gout	1		Teeth	121
Grief	3		Thrush	5
Gripes	51		Timpany	1
Jaundies	5		Tissick	11
Imposthume	11		Vomiting	3
Infants	16		Wind	3
Kild by a ffall from the Belfrey at Alhallows the Greate	1		Wormes	15

CHRISTNED { Males 95, Females 81, In all 176 }   BURIED { Males 4095, Females 4202, In all 8297 }   PLAGUE 7165

Increased in the Burials this Week — 607

Parishes Clear of the Plague — 4   Parishes Infected — 126

The Assize of Bread, A Penny Wheaten Loaf to contain Nine Ounces and a halfe.

OPPOSITE
Bills of mortality for the
week 12–19 September
1665. The parish of St
Dionis is listed in column
2, line 2. 126 parishes were
infected with the plague
and the official number of
plague deaths in the week
was given as 7,165

of the parishioners of St Dionis, and fled to the country. Rawlinson survived the epidemic of 1665 but his household succumbed a year later, forcing the closure of The Mitre once again, and in September 1666 the tavern was ruined by the Great Fire. Ever resourceful, Rawlinson rebuilt it, resuscitated his business and lived to enjoy his year as Master of the Vintners' Company (1678–9).

Social activities ceased while the plague was at its height between the months of June and September 1665. The Ironmongers' Company cancelled its customary dinners for several months and only the determined turned up for meetings at the hall, Geffery among them. Somehow the Clerk, Thomas Heatley, 'guarded' the hall against the plague, earning himself a gratuity of £15.[63] Although there were too few members at the August meeting to constitute a Court, those present resolved to send £20 to the City Chamberlain for the relief of the poor 'with ye contagion'.[64] As Deputy of Lime Street Ward and Junior Warden of the Ironmongers' Company, Geffery considered it was his duty to remain in the City throughout the plague so as to enforce the litany of orders that emanated from the Court of Aldermen. These included the miserable job of shutting infected people in their houses whereupon a red cross was painted on the front door, with the pitiful inscription 'Lord have mercy upon us'.

Geffery and his wife managed to avoid the plague. People were advised to ward off infection by the use of vinegar, smoking or chewing tobacco, munching garlic and rue and indulging in concoctions from the apothecary. They were advised to keep coal fires burning in their homes and at their gates, even though this was summer (it was believed that fire eliminated the infectious particles), while mountainous civic bonfires burned for days and nights at the Royal Exchange and on the corner of Leadenhall Street with Gracechurch Street.

THE GREAT FIRE OF LONDON

The Great Fire broke out in Pudding Lane at one o'clock in the morning on 2 September 1666 and, fanned by an easterly wind, it destroyed some 13,200 houses, eighty-seven parish churches, St Paul's Cathedral, the Custom House, the Sessions House, the Royal Exchange, fifty-two livery company halls, gaols, bridges, the City gates, shops, warehouses and their contents. The flames reached Geffery's parish church, St Dionis, on the 4th, advancing northwards to Pewterers' Hall and Geffery's mansion. As the flames roared up Lime Street towards Leadenhall, locals made heroic efforts to save the ancient market building that was crucial to the City's food supply and economy. Geffery's house, a warehouse used by the merchant, Peter Hoet, and properties belonging to a Dutchman, Lewen Vandermarsh, marked a turning point. The flames were deflected by water from the parish pump, demolitions and by the initiative of an Alderman (presumably Sir Richard Ryves, Alderman of Lime Street Ward 1661–71), who persuaded anybody he could find to fight the fire, bribing them with a hatful of money. Geffery, Ryves's Deputy and an authoritative, able-bodied man in his fifties, would have been there, fighting the fire to prevent it spreading further north. Vandermarsh adopted the same approach as Ryves, appearing on the scene with £50 in hand to bribe fire-fighters. Vandermarsh ordered the demolition of his own house so as to create a firebreak and this proved effective – part of his house survived, although damaged by water. Geffery's house had to be rebuilt, likewise Richard Briggenshaw's properties, a few paces north of Geffery's (Briggenshaw's properties were sold to the East India Company in 1717 and the site is now part of Lloyds of London).

The abating of the wind, the strength of construction and personal initiative saved some of the City's buildings from the flames. The substantial stone walls of Guildhall remained standing (although severely damaged); Ironmongers' Hall was defended by the Clerk and his cohorts, and the formidable walls of Leadenhall Market repulsed the flames. As Thomas Vincent reported, 'A check it had at Leadenhall by that great building; a stop it had in Bishopsgate, Fenchurch Street, Lime Street, Mark Lane and towards the Tower' on 5 September.[65] By Thursday 6th the flames were extinguished.

Geffery had signed a new lease of 'ye parish's house in his occupation' in Lime Street four months before the Fire destroyed all or most of it.[66] The smaller dwelling that flanked the gateway to his mansion, also leased from the Rector of St Dionis and previously occupied by the apothecary, Michael Markland, was destroyed; a third house in Lime Street leased by Geffery may have survived the flames. In those few days of early September 1666, the Great Fire consumed Geffery's home in Lime Street, a property situated in an enclave called Duke Humphreys between Blackfriars Lane and Puddle Dock, and five further properties in Thames Street (probably warehouses). The fire had spread quickly along Thames Street and the riverfront, igniting hay, timber and coal on the open wharves and fuelled by tallow, oil and spirits stored in the warehouses there (the tobacco merchant John Jeffreys was said to have lost stores of imported tobacco-leaf worth £20,000). Assessing the damage, Robert and Priscilla Geffery found themselves without a home, business premises, warehouses or the goods they had contained. The obvious place to take refuge was with Priscilla's family, who lived to the north, in Clerkenwell, while Geffery turned his attention to rebuilding his own properties and those belonging to the Ironmongers' Company as the main priority.

The disastrous events of the first week of September left the Royal Exchange, shops, warehouses and markets in ruins, hence the trade of London was 'shattered

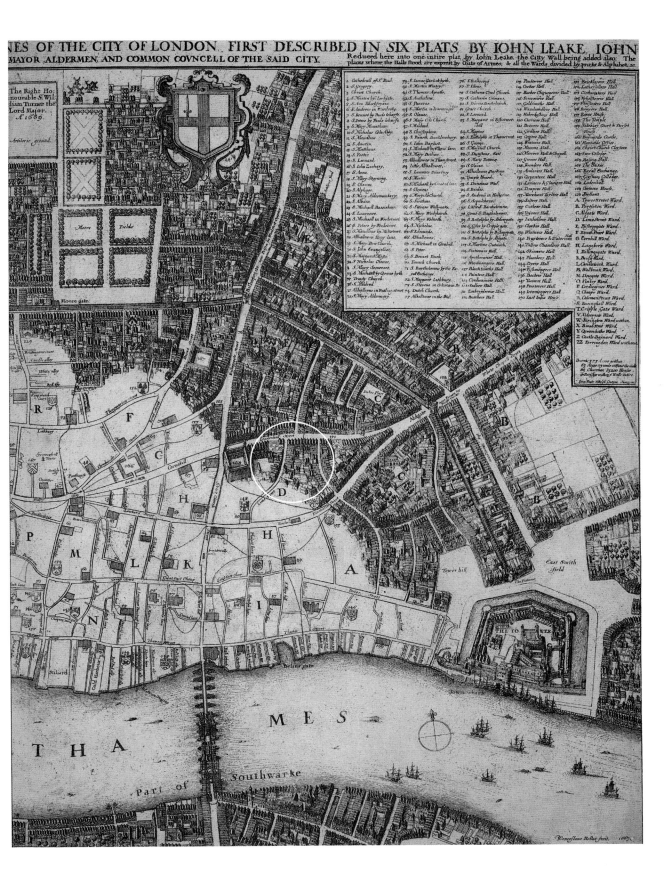

and broken in pieces',[67] affecting merchants, shop-keepers and artisans personally. As the Corporation of London swung into action to repair the damage and restore the economic life of the City, it became clear that a judicial process was needed to oversee the many legal problems that rebuilding the City entailed. Geffery came forward, pressing for a court to be established in order that disputes between landlords and tenants over boundaries, leases and rebuilding costs could be settled quickly and fairly. Thus in January 1667, a committee of a dozen Aldermen and Common Councillors, including Geffery, approached the House of Lords to promote the setting up of the Fire Court, which commenced its proceedings in February and was still settling claims in 1672. Ironically, Geffery was himself summoned to appear before the Court in 1668, over a difference of opinion with the Rector and Churchwardens of St Dionis regarding two houses in Lime Street (the shop formerly leased to Markland, the apothecary, and Geffery's mansion). The Fire Court judges ordered Geffery to rebuild both properties under the terms of a new lease,[68] dating from March 1668 for sixty years.[69] He was obliged to build a substantial house faced in brick, conforming to the Rebuilding Act of 1667. With aspirations to a knighthood and the mayoralty, it seems that Geffery took the opportunity to rebuild the dwellings as one, forming a mansion with sixteen fireplaces or hearths. Peter Hoet was also rebuilding his house in Lime Street and the two neighbours contributed to the cost of resurrecting their parish church, which commenced in 1670.

Remarkably, Ironmongers' Hall in Fenchurch Street was not destroyed by the Great Fire, which was doubly fortunate considering it had recently been repaired and repainted. The survival of the hall was largely due to personal effort: the Clerk, Thomas Heatley, and a shipwright called William Christmas were rewarded with £25 and £4 respectively for their pains – Heatley had transported five barrels of gunpowder from the hall to the Tower of London as a precaution, and the Company's plate and archives had been secreted as the flames approached. Furthermore, Heatley distributed ready money to anyone willing to help him fight the fire.[70] However, other properties belonging to the Company had perished, leaving tenants homeless, and the loss of rents 'by fire' was estimated at £270 15 shillings in a year. As Senior Warden (1666–7), then Master of the Ironmongers' Company for the following year, Geffery was instrumental in finding a tenant for Ironmongers' Hall (the Company retained the use of the reception rooms for meetings and dinners), which partly compensated for the loss of rents from other properties.[71] Geffery also found himself defending the Company's interests in a house in the parish of St Olave, Jewry, that had been destroyed by the fire, bargaining hard at the Fire Court for a fine of £50 to be paid by the tenant for the extension of the lease.[72] As for Geffery's personal interests, he was quick to take advantage of a property in Crutched Friars that belonged to the Company and which had survived the Fire, being on the eastern extremity of the City. After tough negotiation, Geffery obtained a thirty-one-year lease at £30 a year. The sealing of the lease provided the excuse for a celebratory dinner for Geffery and his fellow Ironmongers, who were treated to two legs of mutton, a large sirloin of beef and a shoulder of veal.[73]

REBUILDING AND REVIVAL

In the post-Fire reconstruction of the City, the surveyor Robert Hooke (1635–1703) worked closely with successive Lord Mayors, the Court of Aldermen and Sir Christopher Wren. Geffery first came across Hooke in 1675, in connection with the rebuilding of St Dionis, Backchurch,[74] and in the late 1670s, Hooke and Wren visited St Mary-le-Bow, destroyed in the Great Fire and completed to Wren's designs during Geffery's term as Alderman of Cordwainer Ward, where the church had stood since the late twelfth century. At St Mary-le-Bow, Hooke was involved with the construction of the exceptionally high steeple, which was topped by a dragon weather vane in 1679. The other two churches in Cordwainer Ward were likewise built under Wren's supervision while Geffery was Alderman of the Ward: St Mary Aldermary benefited from the generosity of Henry Rogers of Somerset, and was given a spectacular fan-vaulted ceiling (1679–82), while St Antholin (1678–87) was distinguished by Wren's octagonal plan and oval dome. Within eyeshot of Cordwainer Ward, the new St Paul's Cathedral was also rising from the ruins, opening for services in 1697 but not completed until after Geffery's death.

The Lord Mayor and Aldermen liaised closely with the surveyors over the rebuilding of the City and, as the streets assumed a fresh perspective, a map was needed. Thus John Ogilby and William Morgan produced 'their most accurate survey' of the City, subsidised with £200 from the Corporation of London in 1676. Ogilby died in September 1676, leaving the task of completing their English Atlas project to Morgan, who turned his mind to a new map of London. This ambitious project required financial backing and Morgan petitioned the Court of Aldermen for financial support.[75] The matter was referred to a committee that included Geffery, and having interviewed Morgan, it was decided to give him £50. Geffery may have been instrumental in persuading the Ironmongers' Company to show support for Morgan by purchasing a copy of the 1676 map for £5.[76] This guaranteed that the Company was listed on the *tour de force* produced by Morgan in 1682, *'London &.c. Actually Survey'd'*, which mapped not only the City but also Westminster, Lambeth and Southwark. As one of the

Aldermen who 'bountifully encouraged this Survey and recommended ye First Map of London to the severall Companies for ye use and beautie of their Halls', Sir Robert Geffery's name was inscribed on Morgan's map.[77] Morgan's decorative *oeuvre*, with its inscriptions and engravings of London's most important buildings, represented the revival of the capital under Charles II. It pointed to the City's architectural renaissance (with a vignette of St Paul's Cathedral, still under construction), its mercantile activity (the rebuilt and reopened Royal Exchange) and the resurgence of the loyal Anglican establishment.

The rebuilding and reorganisation of the City's markets stumbled on into the 1680s, and during Geffery's mayoral year, Hooke and his colleague, John Oliver, were still working on plans and regulations for the markets in conjunction with Geffery and the Court of Aldermen. Hooke, doyen of the Royal Society as its Curator of Experiments from 1664 to 1677, contacted Geffery on another matter in 1679 when he applied for funds to enable him to conduct an experiment involving two models and some gunpowder. Geffery and Sir John Shorter (Lord Mayor 1687–8) agreed to the payment of £5 to advance Hooke's experiment. It is intriguing to speculate what Hooke's project might have been. He was working on several ideas at this time: the possibility of human flight (he produced pasteboard models of 'wings' at the Royal Society), the nature of combustion and the design of bullet-proof armour made from quilted silk.[78] Hooke contacted Geffery again in February 1690, and the following year Geffery was among the Aldermen who acknowledged the herculean efforts of Hooke and Oliver as 'surveyors of this City for many years last past' by granting both men the freedom of the City.[79]

'A DREADFULL SPECTACLE'

Robert Geffery's first term as Deputy Alderman for Lime Street Ward (1662–7), could hardly have been more disruptive. Those five years spanned the plague, the Great Fire and the second Anglo-Dutch war, all of which threatened the economy and the very existence of the City. The Great Plague of 1665 and the Great Fire of 1666 were followed by a third catastrophe in the summer of 1667, when the Dutch fleet destroyed the pride of the English navy. The Dutch advanced up the Medway in June, landing 800 men at Sheerness. This generated panic in the City of London, where the alarm was raised by drums sounding in the streets to call out the Trained Bands. It was an emergency to which men of the militia were summoned 'on pain of death to appear in arms tomorrow morning with bullet and powder and money to supply themselves with victuals for a fortnight'.[80] Geffery was instrumental in mustering the men of his Ward, who formed the backbone of the White Regiment (the Red, White, Orange, Yellow, Green and Blue regiments of the Trained Bands accounted for some 10,000 men in all). The City was preparing to defend itself from the enemy, but there was no challenge to the Dutch fleet as it sailed towards Chatham, where the English warships were bombarded. Three men-of-war were annihilated and one was carried off by the enemy. The *Royal James*, the *Royal Oak* and the *Loyal London* were burned (the Ironmongers' Company had contributed to the building of the *Loyal London*, launched only a few weeks prior to the attack). Most humiliating was the capture by the enemy of the flagship of the King's fleet, the *Royal Charles*. The audacity of the Dutch struck Pepys to the heart,[81] while John Evelyn, who went to inspect 'what Mischiefe the Dutch had don', was appalled. As he noted in his Diary, this was 'a Dreadfull Spectacle as ever any Englishmen saw & a dishonour never to be wiped off'.[82]

Scholar, horticulturalist, author and founder member of the Royal Society,

John Evelyn was an investor in the East India Company, like Geffery, and he was well-known to merchants and liverymen of the City through his association with the Royal Mint, Gresham College and committees of the Corporation. One of Evelyn's many contacts, who must have been a member of the Ironmongers' Company, invited him to the Ironmongers' 'fraternity feast' in 1671, when Past Master Geffery and other senior members of the Court were the hosts. Evelyn was bemused by the solemn procession and the sight of 'stewards' with 'garlands about their heads & musique playing before them'.[83]

The destruction wrought by the Dutch on the English fleet in 1667 was a national disaster. Londoners, some of whom had smelled the smoke as the country's finest warships were set alight, spoke of betrayal, and railed at the King and his advisers. At the Royal Exchange, merchants heard that the Dutch were seizing English ships bound for the Far East and taking prisoners. In the back streets, gossip dwelt on the scandalous dishonesty of the Lord Mayor, Sir William Bolton, who had misappropriated charitable funds, cheating the poor of some £1,800 – 'the greatest piece of roguery that they say was ever found in a Lord Mayor'.[84] Reflecting on the past year, Samuel Pepys despaired, 'there being little hopes left but that the whole nation must in a very little time be lost, either by troubles at home, the Parliament being dissatisfied and the King led into unsettled counsels... or else by foreign invasion to which we must submit'.[85] Pepys concluded his depressing comments on the past year by making his will. Robert Geffery, on the other hand, was optimistic, applying his prodigious energy to the problem of rebuilding and reviving the City, and revelling in his role as Master of the Worshipful Company of Ironmongers.

THE MASTER

As a liveryman from 1646, Geffery had made himself useful to the Ironmongers' Company by serving on committees, auditing the accounts and acting as a viewer and searcher of Ironmongers' shops. His potential for high office became clear when, at the Restoration of King Charles II in 1660, he was selected as one of the 'most gracefull, tall and comely personages... every one of them to be well horsed and in their best array or furniture of velvit (plush or satten) and chains of gold' to receive the King as he rode into the City on 29 May.[86] After his years in exile, this was the day Charles II took possession of his kingdom, and Londoners rejoiced to see the monarch process through the streets on his birthday; 20,000 men were on parade, mounted and on foot, brandishing swords and shouting for joy. The streets were strewn with flowers, fountains flowed with wine, and the crowds were so numerous that the procession took

OPPOSITE
An illustration of a 'garland' or cap, as worn by Geffery when Master of the Ironmongers' Company. It was made of crimson velvet (green for the Wardens) and adorned with the arms and crest of the Company engraved on silver plates and enamelled. Salamanders were incorporated into the coat of arms in 1455 (salamanders were said to be able to withstand fire, an allusion to the strength of iron)

seven hours, 'and all this without one drop of bloud & by that very army, which rebell'd against him'.[87] Two years later, in August 1662, the Lord Mayor ordered the Ironmongers' Company to take part in the river procession 'with as much glory as possible',[88] to greet King Charles II and Queen Catherine of Braganza, who had been married in May (see pages 66–7). The royal couple were rowed from Hampton Court to take up residence at Whitehall Palace, and despite the fact that Catherine was a Roman Catholic and Portuguese, the City presented a spectacular show of pageants and ceremonial barges (Catherine brought with her a large cash dowry, also Tangier and Bombay). Later that year Geffery was one of the posse of Ironmongers 'well-mounted and in velvet coates' escorting the Russian ambassador to his lodging in the Strand.[89] He could be relied upon to appear at ceremonial events appropriately dressed and horsed, a handsome figure with a commanding presence.

Following the Restoration of the monarchy in 1660, trading activities received a stimulus and Geffery played a part by ensuring that the standards of trading Ironmongers were maintained, and by training apprentices. As a viewer and searcher, he patrolled Ironmongers' shops, inspecting goods for quality, weight and price on the appointed search days. One of his less pleasant duties was the payment of £2,000 to the City Chamberlain as the Ironmongers' 'loan' to finance the Dutch war (1664). With an impressive record of service to his Company, his Ward and his parish, and in view of his steady promotion from apprentice to liveryman, from Junior Warden to Senior Warden, his election as Master of the Ironmongers' Company was predictable.

Thus on election day, 4 July 1667, Robert Geffery was chosen Master of the Ironmongers' Company, with Joseph King and William Hinton as his supporting Wardens. The installation of the new officers was marked by a service at All Hallows, Staining, followed by a feast at Ironmongers' Hall, when the Master and Wardens wore their gowns and the 'garlands' of office, which were in fact circular velvet hats (crimson for the Master, green for the Wardens) adorned with the arms and crest of the Company.[90] Geffery now took the lead in all Company

The Triumphall Entertainment of ÿ King and Queenes Ma:ties by ÿ Right hon:ble ÿ Lord Maior and Cittizens of London at their coming from Hampton-court to Whitehall (on ÿ River of Thames) Aug: ÿ 23 1662. Aqua

To the right Hon:ble S:r Iohn Frederick K.t Lord Maior of ÿ Citty of London and to his right &c: the Masters, Wardens, Assistants, & Liueryes, of ÿ first 12 (and all other ÿ Companies, of that &c.

business, presiding over Court meetings, hosting ceremonies and entertainments at Ironmongers' Hall and representing his Company in the City. Fellow Ironmongers addressed him reverently as 'Master' and he enjoyed an assured place in London society, along with the other Masters of the 'Great Twelve', many of whom were wealthy overseas merchants. The year 1667 to 1668 was a challenging one for the Master of a livery company: the City was still a building site and many of its inhabitants had lost their homes and livelihoods in the Great Fire. Under Geffery's chairmanship, meetings of the Court of the Ironmongers' Company reflected the difficulties inherent in a massive rebuilding project – desperate tenants, boundary disputes, new leases and rents had to be dealt with.

Gradually, future prospects brightened. The Treaty of Breda, signed in July 1667, gave a respite from war against the Dutch and in October of that year, King Charles II laid the first stone of the first pillar of the new Royal Exchange, signalling the revival of London as a trading mecca (the Exchange opened for

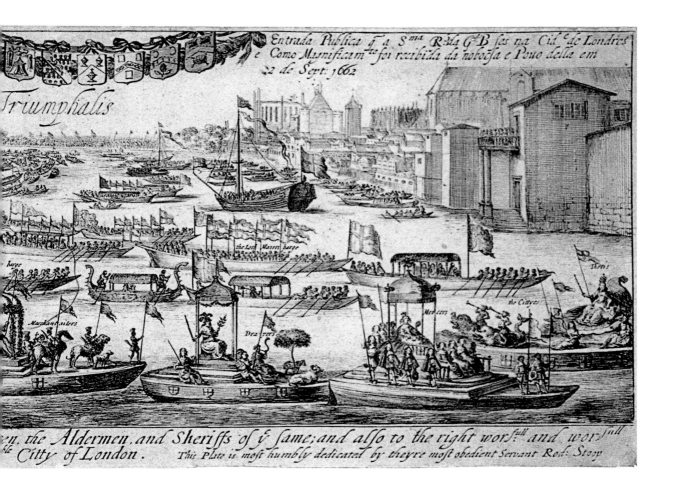

Aqua Triumphalis by Dirck Stoop depicts the arrival at Whitehall Palace of Catherine of Braganza and King Charles II, 23 August 1662, following their marriage. The Ironmongers participated in the celebrations; the Company's coat of arms are at the top, third from right

trading two years later). Geffery was personally involved in the rebuilding and revival of London, pressing for the Fire Court to be established, rebuilding his own house and warehouses, negotiating with Wren and his surveyors in relation to St Dionis, Backchurch, and masterminding the rebuilding and leasing of the Ironmongers' properties. With the reconstruction of the burned City in hand, Geffery was keen to expand his overseas trading activities, so he recruited three apprentices in 1668: John Younge, Robert Scawen and George Sowton (his great nephew, who was eventually made a freeman of the Ironmongers' Company in 1703, so maintaining a family connection with the Company). At the close of his year as Master, Geffery was clearly planning to consolidate his business interests, little suspecting that he would be called upon to serve a second term as Master by command of King James II in 1685, the year that also saw him appointed Lord Mayor of London.

ENDNOTES

1 The Skinners and Merchant Taylors vie for the position of the sixth/seventh livery company, a situation described as being 'at sixes and sevens' **2** CMIC, 22 September 1646, GL MS. 16967/5 **3** Ibid., 13 June 1643, GL MS. 16967/4 **4** Nicholl, pp.231–2 **5** CMIC, 29 April 1645, GL MS. 16967/4 **6** *The Letters of John Paige, London Merchant 1648–1658*, ed. by George F. Steckley (1986), p.14 **7** CMIC, 29 April 1645, GL MS. 16967/4 **8** Nicholl, Appendix XVII, p.XXVIII **9** Ibid., p.XXXI **10** Walker presented a copy of a book by Andrew Willet, *Synopsis Papismi. A General view of Papistry* (1634), to the Company in 1681 with a personal inscription, see Nick Poyntz, 'Henry Walker – a glimpse of a Company member's life in the mid-17th Century', *Annual Report 2010–2011*, The Worshipful Company of Ironmongers (2011) **11** CMIC, 16 January 1649 and 8 August 1654, GL MS. 16967/5 **12** JE, vol II, 2 May 1643, p.81 **13** The Company's Ordinances of 1498 specified four Quarterly Courts, originally for the whole fellowship. In practice, the Master, Wardens and interested liverymen participated. The Court was constituted separately from the livery in 1978 **14** CMIC, 18 January 1648, 18 January 1653, 21 January 1658, 28 May 1658, GL MS. 16967/5 **15** Ibid., 6 February 1654 **16** JE, vol III, 8 February 1654, p.93 **17** Marriage Registers, Mercers' Company Archives, Mercers' Hall, London **18** Luke Cropley's will, 2 April 1662, PRO/PROB11/307, TNA **19** Figures derived from E.H. Phelps Brown and Sheila V. Hopkins, 'Seven centuries of the prices of consumables compared with builders' wage rates', *Economica*, November 1956, and the UK Retail Price Index 2012, www.wolfbane.com/rpi **20** Luke Cropley's will, op.cit. **21** John Stowe, *Survey of London* (1598), rev. edn. 1980, p.242 **22** Horton was a member of the Mercers' Company. The incumbent of St Mary, Colechurch, usually officiated at the Mercers' Chapel **23** Nicholl, Appendix XX, p.XLVI and note **24** John Stowe, op. cit., p.136 **25** Betty Masters, *The Public Markets of the City of London surveyed by William Leybourn in 1677* (1974) **26** Lease, 20 January 1673, COL/CCS/RM16/0072–010, LMA. This site adjoined another in the tenure of Geffery. In April 1700 Geffery signed the lease of two dwelling houses 'abutting his dwelling house on the east', COL/CCS/RM16/35/32, LMA **27** 23 September, 11 December 1675, ME/441 and 330, CRO **28** An inventory of Alderman Abdy's house in Lime Street (1640) provides a good example of an Alderman/merchant's house of the period, MS. 3760, LMA **29** William D. Cooper, 'St Dionis Backchurch', *Transactions London and Middlesex Archaeological Society* (1875), vol IV, pp.201–23 **30** St Dionis Vestry Minutes, Easter 1652, MS. 4215/1, LMA **31** Hearth tax assessment 1672, COL/CHD/LA/03/025/009/022 and /029, LMA **32** Executors' Accounts, 1707, C9/332/55, TNA. These were produced at a Court of Chancery case, Ironmongers' Company v. Roberts. In 1695 Geffery's house was inhabited by himself, Katherine Geffery, Thomas Senior and three female servants, see Assessments, St Dionis, Backchurch, 1695, COL/CHD/LA/04/0/1/028, LMA **33** SP, vol V, 8 January 1664, pp.9–11. Pepys estimated that the hanging of Turner was watched by some 12–14,000 people **34** Thomas de Laune, *The Present State of London* (1681), pp.350–3 **35** John Strype, *A Survey of the Cities of London and Westminster* (1720), vol I, pt 2, p.89 **36** Survey of 1847 by Richard Suter (1853), SC/GL/PR/350/LIM, LMA, also plans of parish properties 9,10,11 Lime Street, 1884, based on a lease of 1875, P69/DIO/D/107, MS. 12,183, LMA **37** 4 December 1684, Rep 90, LMA **38** John Mills and Peter Oliver, *The Survey of Building Sites in the City of London after the Great Fire of 1666* (1967), vol I, pp.12, 43, 76 and vol V, p.128V **39** *Calendar of Treasury Books 1685–1689*, prepared by W.A. Shaw (1923), vol III, pt 2, p.555 **40** CMIC, 11 June 1658, GL MS. 16967/5 **41** Executors' Accounts, op. cit. Figures derived from the Phelps Brown and Hopkins Index and UK Retail Price Index 2012, see note 19 above **42** J. Polsue, *A Complete Parochial History of the County of Cornwall* (1868), rev. edn. 1974, vol II, p.397 **43** D-D/6/40–41 and D-D/8/115, Centre for Buckinghamshire Studies **44** Lime Street Ward Poor Contributions, MS. 1169/1, LMA **45** *A Calendar of the Court Minutes of the East India Company 1664–1667*, ed. by Ethel B. Sainsbury and Sir William Foster (1925), p.360 **46** SP, vol III, 22 March 1662, p.50 **47** Ibid. Pepys's spelling of Geffery (Jefferys) was one of many variations. It has raised the question that Pepys might have been referring to the tobacco trader John Jeffreys (c.1614–88) or his nephews, Sir Jeffery Jeffreys (c.1652–1709) and John Jeffreys (c.1659–1715). But John Jeffreys senior was a bachelor so would not have toasted his wife's health. His nephews were too young to have been present at this meeting **48** *A New Dictionary of the Terms, Ancient and Modern of the Canting Crew* (c.1699). See also Ned Ward, *The London Spy* (1698–1700), rev. edn. 1993, p.343, where fumbler is defined as a sexually impotent man **49** St Dionis Churchwardens' Accounts,1654, f.102, MS. 4215/1, LMA **50** St Dionis Vestry Minutes, 10 June, 14 August 1667, MS. 4216/1, LMA **51** Ibid., 6 April 1670, 27 April 1671 **52** St Dionis Churchwardens' Accounts, 18 February 1702, MS. 4215/1, LMA **53** SP, vol I , 16 September 1660, p.245 **54** SP, vol IV, 25 December 1664, p.356 **55** St Dionis Vestry Minutes, 24 October 1666, 3 April 1667, 31 March 1670, MS. 4216/1, LMA **56** Ibid., 4 December 1672 and St Dionis Churchwardens' Accounts, 7 January 1672, ff.161–6 et seq, MS. 4215/1, LMA **57** St Dionis Vestry Minutes op.cit., 12 October 1683, f.107 and 19 March 1684, f.115 **58** St Dionis Churchwardens' Accounts, 1659, f.114, MS. 4215/1, LMA **59** Ibid., April 1676, January 1677, MS. 4215, ff.189,191, LMA. For a description of the church and its benefactions see John Strype, *A Survey of the Cities of London and Westminster and the Borough of Southwark* (1754), vol I, pp.476–82 and Wren Society, *The Parochial Churches of Sir Christopher Wren* (1933), vol X, pt 2, pp.24–5 **60** St Dionis Vestry Minutes, 13 April 1705, MS. 4216/2, LMA **61** E. Hatton, *A New View of London* (1708), vol I, p.212 **62** *A Collection of the Yearly Bills of Mortality 1657–1758* (1759) **63** CMIC, 5 July 1666, GL MS. 16967/6 **64** Ibid., 4 August 1665, GL MS. 16967/5 **65** Thomas Vincent, *God's Terrible Voice in the City* (1667), p.57 **66** St Dionis Vestry Minutes, 26 May 1666, MS. 4216/1, LMA **67** Thomas Vincent, op. cit., p.58 **68** Philip E. Jones, *The Fire Court. Calendar of the Judgements and Decrees* (1970), vol II, pp.46–7 **69** St Dionis Vestry Minutes, 31 March 1670, MS. 4216/1, LMA **70** CMIC, 14 September 1660, GL MS. 16967/5 **71** Ibid., 22 November 1666, GL MS. 16967/6 **72** Philip E. Jones, op. cit., p.41 **73** CMIC, 12 August 1667, GL MS. 16967/6. In 1669 Geffery assigned his lease of the house in Crutched Friars to William Dale **74** R.T. Gunther, *Early Science in Oxford. The Life and Work of Robert Hooke* (1935), vol X, includes Hooke's diary for 1688–90. See also *The Diary of Robert Hooke 1672–80*, ed. by Henry W. Robertson (1935), p.90 **75** April 1677, Rep 82. See also *The A to Z of Restoration London*, introduction by Ralph Hyde, London Topographical Society (1992) **76** Nicholl, p.286 **77** William Morgan, *London &c. Actually Survey'd* (1682), reproduced with an introduction by Ralph Hyde (1977). See also *The A to Z of Charles II's London 1682*, London Topographical Society (2013). Geffery may have been influential in recruiting the support of the East India Company, the Royal African Company and the Levant Company who also 'encouraged this worke' **78** Miscellaneous papers, 8 April 1679, COL./CHD/CM/07/024, LMA **79** 8 December 1691, Rep 96 **80** SP, vol VIII, 11 June 1667, p.260 **81** Ibid., 12 June 1667, p.261 **82** JE, vol III, 28 June 1667, p.486 **83** JE, vol III, 21 September 1671, p.587. Evelyn refers to four 'stewards' choosing their successors, inferring this was the election day feast, but that was usually held in July **84** SP, vol VIII, 3 December 1667, p.562 **85** Ibid., 31 December 1667, p.602 **86** Precept from Lord Mayor, 17 May 1660, Nicholl, p.274 and CMIC, 22 May 1660, GL MS. 16967/4 **87** JE, vol III, 29 May 1660, p.246 **88** CMIC, 20 August 1662, GL MS. 16976/5 **89** Ibid., 26 October 1662 **90** The Master and Wardens of several livery companies, e.g. the Leathersellers, still wear their ancient 'garlands' on ceremonial occasions. The Ironmongers' 'garlands' cannot be found

An ELEVATION, PLAN, and HISTORY, of the Royal Exchange of LONDON.

10

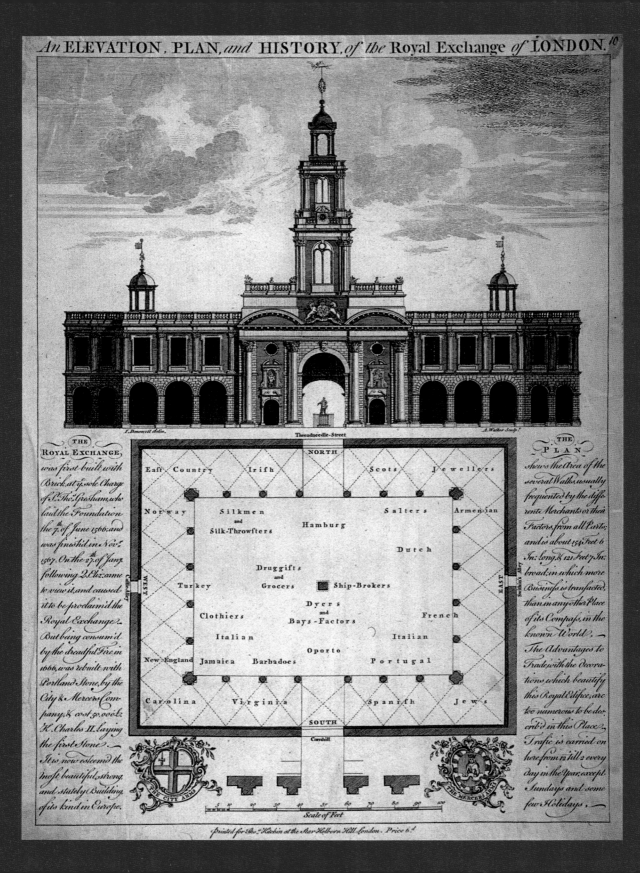

I. Donowell delin.

Threadneedle-Street

A. Walker Sculp.

THE ROYAL EXCHANGE

was first built with Brick, at ij. sole Charge of Sr. Thos. Gresham, who laid the Foundation the 7th of June 1566: and was finish'd in Novr. 1567. On the 27th of Janry. following Q. Eliz: came to view it, and caused it to be proclaim'd the Royal Exchange. But being consum'd by the dreadful Fire in 1666, was rebuilt with Portland Stone, by the City & Mercers Company, & cost 50.000£. K. Charles II. Laying the first Stone. It is now esteem'd the most beautiful, strong, and stately Building of its kind in Europe.

THE PLAN

shews the Area of the several Walks usually frequented by the different Merchants or their Factors, from all Parts; and is about 154 Feet 6 In: long, & 121 Feet 7 In: broad; in which more Business is transacted, than in any other Place of its Compass, in the known World. The Advantages to Trade, with the Decorations which beautify this Royal Edifice, are too numerous to be describ'd in this Place. Trafic is carried on here from 12 till 2 every day in the Year, except Sundays and some few Holidays.

NORTH

East Country — Irish — Scots — Jewellers

Norway — Silkmen and Silk-Throwsters — Hamburg — Salters — Armenian

Dutch

WEST — Turkey — Druggists and Grocers — Ship-Brokers — EAST

Clothiers — Dyers and Bays-Factors — French

Italian — Italian

New England — Jamaica — Barbadoes — Oporto — Portugal

Carolina — Virginia — Spanish — Jews

SOUTH

Cornhill

THE CITY ARMS

THE MERCERS ARMS

Scale of Feet

Printed for Thos. Kitchin at the Star Holborn Hill London. Price 6d.

3 | INTERNATIONAL MERCHANT

As part of his apprenticeship, Robert Geffery was trained in the basics of ironmongery and introduced to book-keeping and stock-taking. He would have accompanied his master, Richard Peate, to markets and warehouses, found his way around the City and made contacts among the merchant community. On being granted the freedom of the Ironmongers' Company in 1637, Geffery may have become Peate's partner, as the springboard to an independent career. In the inclement economic circumstances of the time, this would have been a prudent decision for the elderly Richard Peate and his protégé, Robert Geffery.

During the 1650s Geffery made his own way as a married man, a worthy citizen of Lime Street Ward, a diligent parishioner and an overseas merchant. Taking advantage of the strong connections between the Ironmongers' Company and the Levant Company, he joined the latter in 1653; the following year he signed a petition for greater freedom for members of the East India Company to trade for themselves, indicating ambition if not experience. From modest beginnings as an apprentice to a Master Ironmonger and some experience in the trade, Geffery's interests expanded during the post-Restoration period. In 1663 he was exporting English cloth to Leghorn (Livorno, Italy) aboard the *Anne and Christopher* and the following year he sent bales of serge (a hard-wearing woollen cloth) with the *Golden Fleece* to Leghorn via Gibraltar.[1] During the 1670s, he was profiting from the triangular international trade between England, West Africa and the Caribbean through membership of the Royal African Company. From the 1680s he was a joint owner of the *China Merchant*, a ship that undertook voyages to West Africa to collect gold, ivory and slaves, transporting the enslaved Africans to Barbados and returning to England with extremely valuable cargoes of gold, 'elephants' teeth' (ivory tusks) and sugar. Geffery also imported currants, cotton calico, and wines for the King.

Geffery established a reputation as a good and honest citizen who served his parish, Ward and livery company dutifully; he was an excellent magistrate, sociable and extrovert by nature. His personal qualities and wide interests meant that he could rely on contacts in the key City institutions – at Guildhall, the Custom House, in the overseas trading companies, the livery companies and at the Royal Exchange, where merchants, ships' captains and travellers from abroad congregated to exchange news, the latest prices and gossip. For

London merchants, 'the Change' was as central to their lives as Westminster was for lawyers, or Smithfield for butchers. Geffery was to be found there, pacing the Turkey Walk in the quadrangle where he met fellow merchants of the Levant Company; he would have listened to the foreign merchants' news and gleaned information about prices, ships and prospects for trade. He may then have used the services offered by scriveners and notaries, before making purchases in the small shops called pawns in the galleries of the upper floor where women sold millinery and small dealers supplied tea, spectacles and haberdashery.

PREVIOUS PAGE
Elevation, plan and history of the Royal Exchange by John Donowell, c.1750. As a member of the Levant or Turkey Company, Geffery frequented the Turkey Walk on the west side of the quadrangle

LEFT
Portrait of Nicholas Leate (1565/6–1631), by Daniel Mytens the elder. The painting was presented to the Ironmongers' Company by his sons, Richard and Huet, in 1631 'as a token of their love to remain in the Hall as a remembrance of their dear deceased father'

The Turkey Company

The Levant or Turkey Company was the *grande dame* of England's overseas trading companies, having been incorporated in 1581 (the Muscovy Company pre-dated it, but lost its monopoly in 1698). During the seventeenth century, Turkey merchants, as they were called, were strongly represented in the membership of the Ironmongers' Company and Geffery benefited from the close ties between the livery company and the trading company. The Levant Company was a regulated enterprise, whose members paid a fee to obtain the freedom to trade under its auspices and who supported it by a levy on their personal trade to the area covered by the Company's monopoly. In the second half of the seventeenth century, when Geffery became involved with the Company, cloth, tin, lead, pewter, calico, spices, indigo, sugar, pepper and 'brazile wood' (wood of a tree native to the East Indies which yielded a red dye) were the chief exports to Turkey and the Mediterranean (the exotic goods having first arrived in London from Asia). These exports were exchanged for raw silk, gems, wine, carpets, drugs, oils and, above all, currants, which were shipped to London from the Levant Company's ports at Constantinople, Smyrna, Aleppo and elsewhere in the Mediterranean. The Company's ships usually sailed to the Mediterranean four times a year, escorted by the King's fleet in times of war. Each ship was manned by between fifty to eighty men and boys and equipped with arms and munitions. The Governor, Deputy Governor, Husband and Assistants in London decided when and how many ships sailed, set the charges for freight and appointed consuls (sometimes referred to as ambassadors) at the ports. Within this framework, the individual merchant traded using his own capital, exporting the goods of his choice and importing commodities such as carpets, currants and oils.

Ties between the Levant Company and the Ironmongers' Company dated from 1592, when Nicholas Leate (1565/6–1631), who was Master of the Ironmongers three times between 1616 and 1628, became a Turkey merchant; and when the Levant Company's charter was confirmed in 1605, Leate was one of its eighteen Assistants (directors).[2] His network of servants and factors in Turkey and France formed the basis of an immensely profitable import/export business and for plant-gathering. These contacts abroad enabled Leate to indulge his passion for horticulture by collecting seeds and exotic plants such as the Syrian double yellow rose and the Persian lily, which were exported from Constantinople to London, to the delight of English botanists such as John Gerard and John Parkinson. Leate's interests extended to many spheres, his advice was sound and the merchants of London took note of the profits he made. He died while Geffery was still an apprentice, but his fame was legendary and his portrait (presented by his two sons) was hung at Ironmongers' Hall, where it remains.

Geffery may also have been inspired by Thomas Mun, a shrewd economist, whose book, *England's Treasure by Foreign Trade* (1624 with many later editions), encouraged young men to seize the new opportunities for trade, particularly with Turkey and Asia. Another author who extolled overseas trade was Lewes Roberts, a member of the Levant Company who had served at Constantinople (he was the father of Gabriel, chief executor of Geffery's will). Roberts's *Merchant's Map of Commerce* (1638) provided all the information a merchant needed, including maps, details of currencies and the appropriate commodities for trading with Turkey, Africa, Asia and America. Lewes Roberts and his sons, Nicholas Leate and his sons, Sir Thomas and Sir James Cambell, Sir Andrew Riccard and Sir Christopher Clitherow were leaders of the mercantile milieu of the City of London, who would have influenced Geffery's career.

The Ironmonger/Levant Company link was fortified by two Clerks to the Ironmongers' Company who doubled as book-keepers to the Levant Company. Ralph Hanson/Handson (Leate's cousin), was Clerk from 1619 to 1654, and Thomas Heatley (father-in-law to another merchant-Ironmonger, Thomas Carew) succeeded Hanson in both roles – together they served the Ironmongers' Company for a total of seventy-five years. In the second half of the seventeenth century the number of Ironmongers who traded through the Levant Company increased, and apart from occasional meetings at Drapers' Hall, Fishmongers' Hall, or at the house of Sir Andrew Riccard in Mark Lane, the Levant Company's Court of Assistants met at Ironmongers' Hall, for a payment of between £6 or £10 into the poor box.[3] Alderman Riccard (1603/4–72), Governor of the Levant Company from 1654 until his death, Deputy Governor of the East India Company during the 1660s and 1670s and an investor in the Royal African Company, was 'one of our ablest merchants', as Pepys recognised.[4] Pepys sat in on a meeting of the Levant Company at Riccard's house in 1665 (due to his position on the Navy Board, Pepys was a linchpin for London merchants who were concerned about the paralysis of trade due to the second Anglo-Dutch war).[5] On his monument, Riccard was described as 'an opulent Merchant of London whose active Piety, inflexible integrity and extensive Abilities alike distinguished and exalted Him in the Opinion of the Wise and Good'.[6]

Pepys and Geffery had friends and interests in common. They had met at the port of London in March 1662 (see page 50); possibly they encountered each other again later that year when Pepys attended the funeral of Sir Richard Stayner (formerly Commander of the fleet at Tangier) which was held at Ironmongers' Hall.[7] They signed the 'Ancient Vellum Book' of the Honourable Artillery Company on the same day in August 1669, and may also have come

OPPOSITE
Portrait of Sir
Christopher Clitherow,
Lord Mayor 1635–6,
attributed to the circle
of Robert Peake

74

across each other at St Dionis, Backchurch, in the company of their mutual friends, Daniel Rawlinson and John Battersby, and through their contacts in the Levant Company. Pepys was familiar with Geffery's church and neighbourhood, and in January 1664 he paid 1 shilling to witness the hanging of 'Colonel' Turner on a gibbet erected at the northern end of Lime Street, a sensational spectacle that cannot have escaped the notice of Robert Geffery.

Among the Master Ironmongers of the second half of the seventeenth century, twenty-one belonged to the Levant Company, compared to eight who were members of the East India Company, four who traded through the Royal African Company and a minority who had links with the Muscovy (Russian) Company, the Eastland or the Hambro trading companies. A list of thirty leading Ironmongers who were 'Turkey and other merchants' in 1689 underlines the Ironmongers' interests in overseas trade.[8] The Ironmonger/Turkey merchants at that date included the Clerk, Thomas Heatley, Robert Geffery, Charles Thorold, Richard Carew, Thomas Betton, John Sandys, Henry Hunt, Thomas Puckle and Edward Randall, and when the Secretary of the Levant Company, Thomas Coke, sought an apprenticeship for his son, he entrusted the boy to an Ironmonger, Ralph Lane.

Geffery's career as a Turkey merchant commenced in September 1653. The formalities were similar to those of a livery company and in Geffery's case he was admitted by redemption (as opposed to patrimony or servitude). He swore the oath and paid the fee at a meeting held in the familiar surroundings of Ironmongers' Hall.[9] For the last year or so, a generally successful war against the Dutch had raised morale and the first of a series of Navigation Acts had the effect of protecting English merchants and ship-owners. City merchants had a strong voice in the foreign and commercial policy-making of Oliver Cromwell's commonwealth, so it was with optimism that Geffery started to trade with Turkey and the Mediterranean countries. There were, of course, financial risks and much depended on the co-operation of the Grand Viziers of the Ottoman Empire and the Governor and Directors of the East India Company. Furthermore, the Levant Company's ships, their cargoes and crews were regularly threatened by the Spanish fleet and by 'Tripoly pyrates' who seized the cargoes and enslaved the crews. The Ironmongers Sir James Cambell (d. 1642) and Thomas Betton (c.1675–1724) were so concerned about the plight of the captured crews that they left bequests in their wills to facilitate the freeing of British prisoners taken by Turkish and Barbary pirates.[10]

At the Restoration of the monarchy in 1660, Charles II granted a new charter to the Levant Company licensing it and 'none other' to trade 'in or to Venice or Turkey or any other part of the Levant or Mediterranean Seas',[11] and appointing the Earl of Winchilsea (1627/8–1689) as its ambassador at Constantinople. Consequently, the Company and its individual members enjoyed a period of prosperity during the 1660s, when Geffery took on five apprentices, reflecting an upsurge in his personal business activities. As a Turkey merchant of some standing, he could command a minimum of £300 (some £39,000 at 2012 values) for each apprentice he agreed to train.[12]

CURRANTS AND WINE

In the early seventeenth century the staple import of the Levant Company was currants from the Greek islands of Zante and Cephalonia. This did not escape the notice of King James I, who imposed customs duties which merchants found unacceptable. At intervals, the Turkey merchants John Bates, Nicholas Leate and Robert Geffery refused to pay the duties on currants. Bates's case reached the Court of Exchequer in 1606; in 1628 Leate led a raid on the Custom House to retrieve some 5 tons of currants that had been impounded because he would not pay the import tax. Geffery showed equal bravado in 1683 when he was

The Custom House.

reprimanded for refusing to pay duty on 'severall parcells of currans' (he had been smart enough to extricate the currants without payment). Officers of the Levant Company called upon Geffery to pay what was due, and it seems that several other merchants had likewise evaded the impositions. Therefore, officials at the Custom House were instructed not to permit the collection of 'any goods whatsoever for any of those persons',[13] suggesting that these merchants were importing more than just currants. Treasury records for 1686 reveal that Geffery was importing wine, noting that a sum of £3,675 was due to be paid to him (lately Lord Mayor), the Sheriffs and others of the City for wine supplied to the late King Charles II.[14]

In the decade that followed the Restoration of the monarchy in 1660, the Levant trade tripled or quadrupled. Between 1676 and 1678 dividends were as high as 55% and members of the Company were reputed to be the wealthiest merchants in the City. Thereafter came a sharp decline, due to competition from French merchants and the dominance of the East India Company. The seriousness of

The Custom House on the Thames waterfront, by John Dunstall (1670s). Destroyed in the Great Fire, the Custom House was rebuilt to designs by Sir Christopher Wren (1669–71)

the situation led Alderman Sir Gabriel Roberts (1635–1715, shortly to be Deputy Governor of the Levant Company), and his former apprentice, John Verney (1640–1717, who had served the Company in Aleppo), to seek an audience with King Charles II at Windsor in July 1679. Verney complained to the King that the Levant Company 'has become as poor as a courtier' and he claimed that English commerce was ruined. The Company was conducted with good old-fashioned honesty, he attested, paying debts before dividends, 'we cannot have one penny dividend but we pay off our debts that if the Company be broke nobody may be sufferers but those that are of it'.[15] The Company was not 'broke' but its members were indeed suffering.

The decline of the Levant trade continued and the 1690s brought double disaster, firstly in 1690 when the Anglo-Dutch fleet was defeated by Admiral Trouville off Beachy Head, giving the French control of the English Channel and secondly, in 1693 when the entire merchant fleet of some 400 vessels was destroyed or scattered by the French in the Bay of Lagos. When that news reached the Turkey Walk at the Royal Exchange, merchants were ashen-faced and sombre, wondering if the catastrophe signalled the demise of the country's mercantile fleet. But Geffery does not seem to have suffered unduly from the decline in the Levant trade: he was astute enough to spread his assets wide. He could afford to subscribe £1,800 (some £250,000 at 2012 values) to a new issue of East India Company stock in 1691, and he continued to reap profits from voyages of the *China Merchant* (see pages 83–90).

THE EAST INDIA COMPANY

When it was established by Queen Elizabeth I in 1600, the East India Company counted veterans of the Levant Company among its founders – Nicholas Leate for example – and for a while the two companies shared offices, ships and letter-books. The Queen's charter to the Governor and Company of Merchants of London trading to the East Indies was a charter of opportunity for 'adventurers', as the intrepid merchants were known. Membership was by patrimony, apprenticeship or by the purchase of a share in a voyage or stocks. Among the early office-holders was a Robert Jeffries/Jefferies/Jeffreys, a Director and auditor (1619, 1621), raising the possibility that he might have been a relative of Robert Geffery – his grandfather or uncle perhaps, who could have provided an entrée to London's mercantile community (see page 26)?

From 1635 the Court of the East India Company met at Sir Christopher Clitherow's house in Leadenhall Street, around the corner from Lime Street (Clitherow being the Governor from 1638 to 1641), and from 1648 the Company

OLD EAST INDIA HOUSE.

was based at a neighbouring house belonging to Lord Craven, soon known as East India House. Both the Company's headquarters and its warehouses in Leadenhall Market were conveniently situated for Robert Geffery. Indeed when the Company built new premises in the back garden of East India House (for the buying, measuring and packing of cloth and other goods for export), 'out of respect' for Sir Robert, 'a chief magistrate of this City', care was taken to give the building a flat roof, so as not to be 'an annoyance' to Geffery by obscuring light from his premises.[16]

The East India Company was run along autocratic lines that were challenged in the 1650s by Maurice Thomson and sixty dissidents, including Geffery. Thomson was a forceful entrepreneur, a ship-owner and merchant trading in coral, currants, gold and silver bullion, saltpetre, tobacco and slaves. He was the leader of the petitioners who, in 1654, campaigned for greater freedom to trade on their own accounts under the umbrella of the East India Company; this, they claimed would 'much increase navigation and trade'.[17] Thomson's party aspired to use their own ships, stocks, factors and initiative (Thomson nursed an ambitious scheme to colonise Assada, a sugar-producing island west of Madagascar). The Court of Directors of the East India Company dismissed the demands put forward by Thomson and his supporters. Nevertheless, a fresh charter was issued

in 1657 and Thomson was appointed Governor under the new regime, which established the East India Company as a joint-stock endeavour. Instead of investing in one voyage, taking the profit and reinvesting or not, subscribers now invested on a more permanent basis in stocks that were traded at East India House. The subscription raised under the charter of 1657 yielded £739,782 for the Company, to which Geffery contributed £125 (£100 of stock in 1657 was worth £245 in 1677, increasing to as much as £500 by 1683 – some £90,000 at 2012 values).[18] Geffery added to his investment with the Company before selling shares worth £1,000 to Charles Thorold (a fellow Ironmonger) and Henry Johnson in 1670. This sale of shares may have reflected Geffery's frustration over the duties on imported calicoes (see below), or simply a personal requirement to pay for the rebuilding of his properties that had been destroyed by the Great Fire. He later reinvested with the East India Company and at the time of his death in 1704 he owned substantial holdings in the Company (see page 86).

CALICO

The omniscient Nicholas Leate had predicted a boom in calico sales when, in 1619, he reported to the East India Company's Court that he had studied the possibilities for the sale of calico in London. He judged it to be a perfect substitute for linen and that an annual ship-load would yield an excellent profit of 'two-for-one'.[19] Leate's prediction proved correct, although it was slow to reach fruition – it was not until the second half of the century that the demand for calicoes escalated. These textiles, which derived their name from their place of origin, Calicut on the coast of Malabar, were exported from Suryapur (Surat) and later from Fort St George (Madras). Cotton calico, whether plain, coloured, striped or chintz, was a new and popular consumer item in Europe; plain white calico was used for bed-linen and clothes, and the painted and printed cottons known as chintz became fashionable for ladies' gowns, and were soon in demand for bed-spreads, hangings and wall-coverings.[20]

In addition to the expanding European market, quantities of Indian textiles arriving in London were re-exported further afield – 'Guinea cloth', for example, (a blue and white check cloth) was popular in West Africa and the West Indies from the middle years of the seventeenth century. The berthing at the port of London of an East Indiaman with its cargo of cotton textiles, silks, pepper, spices and indigo, created a flurry of excitement in the City as the goods were auctioned either for home consumption or export. Sometimes the calico was damaged during the voyage from India, as in 1665, when the East India Company compensated Geffery and two other merchants for imperfect goods.[21]

THE 'CHINA MERCHANT'

In the mid-seventeenth century the East India Company found that it was more economical to charter ships than to build them. Generally, the policy of chartering East Indiamen proved rewarding to both the Company and the ship-owners; furthermore, the number of East Indiamen sailing the oceans (no less than twenty at any one time) stimulated the development of the shipping industry, insurance, broking and chartering in the City of London. During the 1680s and again in 1700, the East India Company chartered the *China Merchant*, a vessel owned by Robert Geffery, John Jeffreys (a nephew of the tobacco merchant), Nathaniel Warren (ship's captain) and William Warren (son of Sir William, a ship-builder and naval contractor who did business with Pepys).[22]

John Jeffreys (*c.*1614–88, known as 'the Great Smoker' on account of his tobacco importing business), his nephews, Alderman Sir Jeffrey Jeffreys (*c.*1652–1709) and John Jeffreys (*c.*1659–1715), and Robert Geffery were linked by their prominence in the trade and politics of the City. John Jeffreys junior led the syndicate that owned the *China Merchant*; he, his brother and their uncle were the owners of at least ten vessels and they may have included Robert Geffery in their other ship-owning ventures (records cite the names of lead owners only). The elder brother, Sir Jeffrey Jeffreys, and Robert Geffery were evidently personal friends, for Geffery was godfather to Sarah, Sir Jeffrey's daughter. Sir Jeffrey inherited from his uncle a large house in St Mary Axe (later Jeffreys' Square), a short walk from Robert Geffery's house in Lime Street. The younger brother, John Jeffreys, was granted the lease of an Ironmongers' Company property in Great Eastcheap after the Great Fire, probably through Robert Geffery's influence, and was so grateful that he donated money to the Company's poor. The two brothers Jeffreys were given mourning rings and the gift of £10 each in accordance with Robert Geffery's will and they duly attended his funeral at St Dionis, Backchurch, on 10 March 1704 (see page 171).

The *China Merchant* was built (probably at Deptford or Blackwall) to the East India Company's specifications and named with the exploitation of the China trade in mind. At 170 tons, with fourteen to sixteen guns and a crew of between twenty-six and thirty-eight, she was one of the smaller vessels chartered by the East India Company. She proved a trusty ship and was one of the first dozen East Indiamen to sail to China with the purpose of securing a monopoly of trade there – the forerunner of a great armada that was to establish regular trade between England and China.[23] Investing in the *China Merchant* was a brave decision for Robert Geffery. He could not match the immense wealth or mercantile experience of the Jeffreys family, but he clearly had confidence in his friends

OPPOSITE
Two views of an
East Indiaman by Isaac
Sailmaker, c.1685. This
vessel was heavily armed
with over sixty guns

as associate investors and he possessed sufficient funds to allow him to take a gamble. For in addition to the danger of war, pirates, sickness and the hazards of sailing round the Cape of Good Hope, China was an unknown, unexplored territory. Geffery took the risk, joined John Jeffreys's syndicate and profited thereby. Other ship-owners did not do so well – Daniel Defoe for instance, famous as the author of *Robinson Crusoe*, invested in shipping in the 1680s and went bankrupt in 1692. Similarly, the physician, John Radcliffe (1650–1714), lost £5,000 on a failed East India shipping venture in 1692 (he later recovered his losses, enabling him to endow the Radcliffe Infirmary and Radcliffe Library, Oxford).

The *China Merchant*, chartered by the East India Company and under the command of Captain John Utber, was one of four ships embarking for the Far East in September 1681 carrying £14,599 worth of goods, plus £28,000 in silver bullion and coin, in the expectation of reaching China. However the Manchu armies had recently captured Amoy, on the south-eastern coast of China, and foreigners were not permitted entry; consequently the *China Merchant* was beset by difficulties. She was prevented from reaching Amoy, so diverted to 'the Macau Islands' near Hong Kong, where, in August 1682, Utber and his crew were confronted by two 'Tartar Mandarins' and several war-boats from Canton, delivering the message that 'all commerce has been impeded' by order of the Emperor. Despite gifts of violet and scarlet cloth, two cases of ironware and two cases of spectacles, the Mandarins made it clear that the *China Merchant* must not proceed to Amoy.[24] So having purchased raw silks and 'tutanagas' (tutenags, white metal canisters for storing tea), the vessel steered west for Fort St George, and reached the port of London in July 1683.

The second voyage of Geffery's ship was more successful: as soon as the Emperor re-opened Chinese ports to foreign trade, the East India Company was quick to seize the opportunity. The *China Merchant* left England early in 1685 with an interesting and varied cargo: three barbers' cases, thirty-six bales of broadcloth, carpets, muskets, pistols, carbines, nails, sword-blades, six anchors, olibanum (a gum resin), chests of window-glass, coral beads, saddles, cotton-wool and yarn, 344 sticks of sandalwood, chintz, calicoes and thirty barrels of gunpowder. The ship anchored at Surat in May, but the small local boats could not reach her to unload, so she proceeded to Bombay and reached Amoy late in July, where she received a cordial welcome. John Gladman, the ship's 'chief' or 'supercargo' (supra-cargo, the commercial agent in charge of the cargo), was instructed to establish Amoy as 'a footing in China to the honour of our nation and future benefit of the Company'. This he did, presenting the local Mandarin with muskets, sword-blades, pistols and a saddle, and receiving by return a hog, a goat, geese, ducks, flour and pots.[25] Gladman took a house for a factory, charmed the Chinese traders, and his ship remained at anchor for five months in order to establish the first of the Company's trading posts in China. Gladman received meticulous orders from London to sell the cargo, then load a ship-full of silks, satins, velvets, chinaware, lacquerware, fresh China roots, sugar, sugar-candy, copper, alum, cambodium (gamboge, a resin used as a yellow pigment and as a purgative) and 'fresh and good tea well-packed' in tutenag canisters and pots, protected by hay and placed carefully in chests.[26] Tea ('tcha') had recently been introduced to the English market and was a commodity that would dominate trade between London and China in the eighteenth century. This voyage lasted two years and in June 1687, Geffery and the other co-owners of the ship received £2,000 (some £260,000 at 2012 values) from the East India Company as the first instalment of payment for freight and demurrage.[27]

After a refit in India, the *China Merchant* was chartered by the Royal African Company in 1689 (see pages 88–90), returning to serve the East India Company for her last voyage to China (1700–3) with a crew of thirty-eight and a cargo worth £20,923. In 1700 she was bound for Borneo, Chusan and Ningpo in pursuit of Nanking silk and a potential market for English woollen cloths in northern China, but a monsoon forced her to anchor at Amoy in September 1701, where she loaded a cargo for Surat including gold to the value of £3,000 (approximately £394,500 at 2012 values). This was a profitable but unhappy voyage: Captain Francis Hosier faced a mutiny by a dozen of his crew led by the ship's surgeon, Thomas Thackham, who brought 'an action against ye captain', and as a result several seamen were arrested. The final leg of the journey extended as far as Barbados, and when the *China Merchant* returned to Gravesend in April 1703, Hosier received £265 in wages for three years' service.[28]

The owners' total profits from the *China Merchant* are difficult to assess (lack of detail, records missing/damaged) but, in addition to the chartering fee from either the East India Company or the Royal African Company, Geffery received a proportion of the profit on the total freight carried on each voyage and he also made money from his personal quota of calicoes that he had imported from Surat for export to West Africa and the West Indies. At the time of the vessel's first voyage for the East India Company, Geffery held £4,000 of stock in that Company.[29] At the launch of a new issue of joint-stock in 1691, he invested £1,800 (compared to £7,000 invested by the King, and £1,000 by the Duke of Beaufort).[30] A new issue of stock in 1693 did not tempt Geffery, although he clung to his existing investment. When he died in 1704 he left £4,108 in East India Company bonds (including interest) and £2,325 in stock and dividends (£4,000 in 1700 is the approximate equivalent of £525,000 in 2012).[31]

THE ROYAL AFRICAN COMPANY

The Company of Royal Adventurers Trading into Africa was relaunched under a new charter as the Royal African Company in 1672, with Robert Geffery as a charter member and the investor of £400 towards a total of £111,000 raised by subscription. King Charles II, the Duke of York and the Earl of Shaftesbury headed the list of 200 subscribing members, forty-eight of whom were Turkey merchants keen to expand their trading activities to Africa.[32] The Duke of York, later King James II, was Governor of the new Company and he invited its directors to hold their first meetings at Whitehall Palace. Under the 1672 charter, Royal African Company merchants were licensed to buy, sell, trade, barter and exchange slaves, wares and other merchandise in West Africa. The enterprise had the King's blessing and the chief resources of the region proved to be gold, ivory, wax, hides, malaguetta (otherwise known as 'Guinea grains' and used as a spice or medicine), palm oil and slaves. In return, West Africa received goods such as iron, cloth and guns, a large proportion of which was of foreign origin, assembled in London prior to shipment to Africa.

Between 1672 and 1713 the Royal African Company, or the Guinea Company as it was sometimes called, exported goods worth in the region of £1,500,000 from Liverpool, Bristol and London to West Africa in more than 500 ships, and transported some 100,000 enslaved men and women from West Africa to the sugar plantations of the West Indies. This was trade on a large and profitable scale. By the beginning of the eighteenth century, the Company's ships had brought to England 30,000 tons of sugar and sufficient gold to coin half a million guineas (the Guinea Coast gave the coin its name). This trade from English ports to West Africa, the West Indies, North America and back stimulated the development of London as an *entrepôt* for international merchandise and formed the basis of many individual fortunes and for British commercial prosperity as a whole, well into the eighteenth century.

The Royal African Company was a major trading interest of many of Robert Geffery's contemporaries: the Jeffreys family, William Warren, Sir Henry Tulse, Sir Samuel Dashwood, Thomas Heatley (Clerk to the Ironmongers), the Cornishman, George Carew (Master of the Ironmongers' Company 1694–5 and Heatley's executor), Sir Gabriel Roberts and Sir William Gore (both of whom were Geffery's executors). Captain (sometimes referred to as Colonel) William Walker, who supplied pikes to Tangier, Alderman Thomas Lewis and Sir William Pritchard were also involved with the Company. This circle of merchants, several of whom were Ironmongers, Lord Mayors and Aldermen, trusted each other implicitly in business and politics, to their mutual benefit and prosperity.

Geffery's investment of £400 in the Royal African Company indicated he was a man of initiative with the confidence to take a risk based on personal judgement. This investment yielded him an average of 7% a year in dividends (naturally, the dividend was paid in guineas) – not a huge reward. However, Geffery found additional sources of income by exporting cotton calico and through part-ownership of the *China Merchant*, which, while chartered to the Royal African Company, yielded him substantial profits from gold, slaves and ivory. In September 1689 the *China Merchant* and the *Armenian Merchant* (part-owned by the brothers John and Jeffrey Jeffreys) were loading cargoes of cloth, beads, iron bars, pewter, carpets and gunpowder and were insured for £3,000 each by the Royal African Company.[33]

Once the *China Merchant* was loaded, Captain Henry Roberts took his leave of the Royal African Company's Court of Assistants and boarded the vessel, which was bound for the Windward Coast between Cape Mount and Cape Three Points on the corner of West Africa. From there she sailed east to the Gulf of Guinea, anchoring at Cape Coast Castle, the Company's main trading post on what was known as the Gold Coast. The next stage of the voyage was from West Africa to Barbados, where her cargo of slaves was sold for £500 (a pre-arranged price).[34] In any one year the Royal African Company supplied as many as 5,000 slaves to the West Indies, where they were sold for between £5 and £15 a head for a fit young man, more in times of scarcity and war. Conditions on the ships were harsh: the slaves were shackled and supplied with meagre 'negroe provisions' of stockfish, biscuits, brandy, beans and peas. English participation in the Atlantic slave trade dated from the Elizabethan era and continued until prohibited by Act of Parliament in 1807.

In addition to slaves, the *China Merchant* carried rough gold, loaded in West Africa and guarded by the Company's factor while the ship anchored at Barbados. Once 'moulted with the fire' in London, this amounted to 1,869 ounces of eighteen carat gold.[35] This cargo of gold and seventy-seven elephants' tusks from Africa, was supplemented at Barbados by sixty-two casks of sugar and smaller quantities of ginger, logwood and indigo. On safe receipt of the goods in England the profits were shared between the ship-owners and the Company. For this voyage Geffery and the co-owners of the *China Merchant* were paid £3,656 16s 8d as their share of the gold (some £500,000 at 2012 values), with subsidiary payments due for other imports.[36]

Stockholders in the Royal African Company received a bonus issue in 1691, which increased their original capital fourfold. In that year, Geffery was appointed an Assistant of the Company (bringing a gratuity) and he undertook additional responsibilities on the committees for correspondence and shipping. Much of his

OPPOSITE
The Royal African Company traded for commodities along the West African coast from 1672

The document, from the Royal African Company archives (1672), reads: 'The Slaves they purchased are sent, for a Supply of Servants, to all His Majesties' American Plantations which cannot subsist without them'.

And, the second paragraph: 'The Gold and Elephants' Teeth, and other Commodities, which are procured in Africa, are all brought into England. The Gold is always coined in His Majesties' Mint. And the Elephants-Teeth, and all other goods, which the Company receives, either from Africa or the Plantations, in returne for their Negros, are always sold publicly at a Candle' [by auction]

time was taken up by litigation and the Company's financial problems (he was known to be good with figures), as a period of decline set in. Throughout his year as an Assistant, he attended the weekly meetings of the Company's Court which were held at African House in Leadenhall Street (now numbers 42–49). Prior to 1678 the Company had its headquarters at Warnford Court near Throgmorton Street, moving from there to the house in Leadenhall Street leased from the widowed Mrs William Roberts (the deal was a family arrangement masterminded by Sir Gabriel Roberts and Sir Samuel Dashwood, Mrs Roberts's brother-in-law and brother, respectively).[37]

The *China Merchant* made one more voyage for the Royal African Company before reverting to the East India Company. She was loaded in October – November 1692 with a cargo of calicoes, serges, carpets (from Turkey), tallow, gunpowder, pewter, lead bars, iron bars (from Sweden), 341 gallons of brandy, 100 blankets, 1,120 dozen knives (armour, not cutlery), East Indian textiles, cowrie shells (used as currency in Africa), coral, eight chests of old sheets (used by Africans to wrap themselves in to sleep at night) and 3,000 rangoes (beads made in Amsterdam or Venice). Once goods had been unloaded at Cape Coast Castle, slaves and gold were brought aboard, and at Jamaica the 262 men and women were delivered (985 brass rings used to chain them were returned to London).[38] It must have been from this voyage that the owners received payment of £1,539 for imported gold in 1696 (some £196,000 at 2012 values).[39] Profits from his overseas trading ventures prompted Geffery to put in a bid to buy the freehold of the premises in Lime Street where he lived, in 1697. He boasted that he had sufficient funds 'to give as much as any person' for the property, but he was disappointed. The Rector and Churchwardens refused to sell, so Geffery had to be content with the extension of his lease.[40]

The Royal African Company's monopoly was disintegrating in the 1690s due to competition, and the war with France disrupted shipping and trade – the Company estimated it made losses of £400,000 during the eight years of war that ended with the Peace of Ryswick in 1697. Geffery was wise enough to sell £1,600 of stock to Captain Robert Lancashire, another Assistant of the Company, in 1692[41] (keeping some £300 worth).[42] He then retired from active participation in the affairs of the Royal African Company, while retaining his interest in the *China Merchant* and continuing to reap the profits from trading in calico, slaves, ivory and gold.

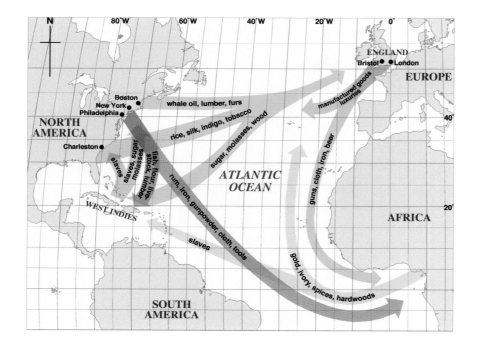

A map showing the triangular trade routes between Britain, Africa, the Caribbean and North America, and the chief commodities traded at the height of the slave trade

ENDNOTES

1 Port Books, E190/50/1 and /2, TNA. 2 Nicholl refers to Leate as an Alderman, incorrectly. Leate was instrumental in draining and developing the marsh outside Aldersgate (1606) which bordered on the site of the present Ironmongers' Hall. 3 Court Minutes, Levant Company, 7 February 1673, SP105/153, TNA. The arrangement came to an end with the death of Heatley in 1694. 4 SP, VOL VIII, 5 April 1667, p.153. 5 SP, vol VI, 23 January 1665, p.20. 6 Inscription on Riccard's monument, St Olave's Church, Hart Street, London. 7 Ibid., vol III, 28 November 1662, p.268. 8 Nicholl, p.336. 9 Court Minutes, Levant Company, 15 September 1653, SP/105/151, TNA. 10 Nicholl, pp.542, 578. 'Barbary' referred to the north African coast and the kingdom of Morocco. 11 Add. MS. 72610, BL. 12 Richard Grassby, *The business community of seventeenth-century England* (1995), p.68. For comparative values, see E.H. Phelps Brown and Sheila V. Hopkins, 'Seven centuries of the prices of consumables compared with builders' wage rates', *Economica*, November 1956, and the UK Retail Price Index 2012, www.wolfbane.com/rpi 13 Court Minutes op. cit., 16 November 1683, 20 June 1684, 26 March 1685, SP105/154, TNA. 14 £96 12s was granted in part payment, see *Calendar of Treasury Books*, prepared by W.A. Shaw (1897–1903), vol III, pt 2, 16 December 1686, p.1078. 15 *Memoirs of the Verney Family* (1899), vol IV, p.258. 16 Court Minutes, East India Company, 3 November 1686, B/38 f.258, BL. See also plans of the site (not entirely accurate) in Sir William Foster, *The East India House. Its History and Associates* (1924), pp.6, 146. 17 *A Calendar of the Court Minutes of the East India Company 1650–1654*, ed. by Ethel B. Sainsbury (1913), p.340. 18 Figures derived from the Phelps Brown and Hopkins Index and the UK Retail Price Index, 2012, see note 12 above. 19 K.N. Chaudhuri, *The English East India Company* (1965), p.194. 20 Chintzes for hangings were first imported into England in 1619. The East India Company's sale of 1626 included 100 pieces for hangings. In 1663 Samuel Pepys bought chintz to line the walls of his wife's study, see John Irwin and Katharine B. Brett, *Origins of Chintz* (1970). 21 *A Calendar of the Court Minutes of the East India Company 1664–1667*, ed. by Ethel B. Sainsbury and Sir William Foster (1925), p.134. 22 There may have been other part-owners of the *China Merchant*. Ships could be owned by a syndicate of four, more usually there were eight or sixteen owners, occasionally thirty-two. 23 Russell Miller, *The East Indiamen* (1980), p.93. 24 East India Company, Factory Records 1615–1703, vol I, G/12/16 ff.67–70, BL. 25 Ibid., G/12/16, f.228. 26 Journal and Diary of John Gladman, ff.297–310, BL. See also East India Company Factory Records, op. cit., vol II, f.216. 27 Court Minutes, East India Company, 3 June 1687, B/39, f.10, BL. The total payment would have been at least double. Inconsistent/damaged/missing records makes it impossible to give a total amount paid per voyage to individual ship-owners. Figures derived from the Phelps Brown and Hopkins Index and UK Retail Price Index, 2012, see note 12 above. 28 Ledger, 'The China Merchant', 1700–03, L/MAR/A/CXLII, BL. 29 Gary S. De Krey, *London and the Restoration 1659–1683* (2005), p.423. 30 East India Company, 18 April 1691, H/1, BL. 31 Executors' Accounts, 1707, C9/332/55, TNA. Figures derived from the Phelps Brown and Hopkins Index and the UK Retail Price Index 2012, see note 12 above. 32 K.G. Davies, 'Joint Stock Investment in the Later Seventeenth Century', *Economic History Review*, vol IV, no 3 (1952), pp.283–301. 33 Court Minutes, Royal African Company, 7 January 1690, and records of the committee of goods, September 1690, T70/127, TNA. 34 Court Minutes, Royal African Company, 17 December 1691, T70/83, TNA. 35 Royal African Company Ledger, 12 February 1691, T70/969, TNA. 36 Ibid., February – November 1691, T70/607, TNA. Figures derived from the Phelps Brown and Hopkins Index and the UK Retail Price Index 2012, see note 12 above. 37 Court Minutes, Royal African Company, 9, 18 July 1678, T70/76, TNA. 38 Royal African Company, goods loaded October – November 1692, T70/1224, TNA. 39 Court Minutes, Royal African Company, 14 January 1696, T70/84, TNA. Figures derived from the Phelps Brown and Hopkins Index and the UK Retail Price Index 2012, see note 12 above. 40 St Dionis Vestry Minutes, 19, 25 May 1697, f.231, MS. 4216/2, LMA. 41 Court Minutes, Royal African Company, 5 January 1692, T70/83, TNA. 42 Executors' Accounts, op. cit.

To all and Singular unto whom thes x
presents shall come J S.r Edward Bysshe K.nt
Clarenceux Principall Herauld & King of Armes
of all y.e South East & West parts of y.e Realme
of England from y.e Riuer of Trent Southward
send Greeting: Wheras S.r Robert Jeffery:
Knight one of y.e Sheriffes of y.e Citty of London
hath desired me to assigne unto him such armes
& Creast as he & his Posterity may Lawfully beare
Know yee therefore y.t J haue thought fit to
assigne unto him y.e Armes hereafter mentioned
(Vizt) Argent Six Billetts Sable on A
Cheife of y.e Second A Lyon Passant. O.r

4 | ARISE, SIR ROBERT

The office of Sheriff is of greater antiquity than any other in the City of London and the counties of England.[1] King Henry I (1100–35) granted the City the right to elect its Sheriffs, and it continues to do so. When Robert Geffery was elected in 1673, it was the custom for the Lord Mayor to indicate his choice of a Sheriff for the forthcoming year by toasting the candidate at a City banquet. Thus it was that Sir Robert Hanson, 'a person who heartily loves the King's interest' raised a gilt cup to Robert Geffery.[2]

At the time of Geffery's election as Sheriff, the euphoria of the Restoration had dissipated and King Charles II's popularity had dipped: his foreign policy was especially unpopular. Shortly before Geffery took office, the army assembled on Blackheath came close to mutiny because the troops thought they were going to have to fight alongside their traditional enemy, the French, against the Dutch – Charles II and Louis XIV had formed an alliance by the 'secret' Treaty of Dover in 1670. The signatories to the Treaty of Dover were Sir Thomas Clifford, Lord Arlington, the Duke of Buckingham, Lord Ashley and Lord Lauderdale (whose combined initials spelt 'CABAL'), but when this powerful team disintegrated and Parliament was prorogued, Charles II pursued his own manifesto. Trusted supporters were promoted to key positions and the King's attitude to the City became increasingly autocratic. Robert Geffery, known to be a royalist, was chosen Sheriff in 1673 and the King conveyed his approval by awarding him a knighthood, immediately and personally.

The year of Geffery's shrievalty, 1673–4, was a watershed in King Charles II's reign. The fiercely anti-Catholic House of Commons reasserted itself, obliging the King to abandon his Declaration of Indulgence and assent to the Test Act of 1673, which forced holders of military and civil offices to swear the oaths of allegiance and supremacy and take communion according to the Anglican rite. Thus the King's brother, the Duke of York, a convert to catholicism, was compelled to resign as Lord High Admiral. Parliament and the people grew increasingly exasperated by King Charles's policies and behaviour: his subjects resented not only his alliance with the French King but also his French mistress, Louise de Kéroualle, who was given the title Duchess of Portsmouth in 1673. From 1676, the year Geffery was elected an Alderman, conspiracies and plots posed the threat of uprisings against the monarch, even the possibility of civil war. Opposition to King Charles and the Duke of York was explicit in the exclusion crisis of 1679–81 which aimed to prevent the Duke from inheriting the throne. The Exclusion Bill failed and the King asserted Stuart supremacy by depriving the City of London, its livery companies and corporations up and down the land of their independent status.

Sheriff Geffery's experience of City politics and institutions was considerable. Between 1659 and his election as Sheriff fourteen years later, he had served as Deputy of Lime Street Ward, Master of the Ironmongers' Company, a Governor of the Irish Society (which oversaw the development of the City's estates in Ulster) and he was auditor of that Society during his shrievalty. His colleague as Sheriff was Sir Henry Tulse, another steady Anglican royalist – as Sir John Robinson reported to the Privy Council, Tulse and Geffery were 'both good men... honest men'.[3] Henceforward, the careers of Geffery and Tulse ran in parallel. They were both knighted by Charles II at Guildhall on 29 October 1673 and over the next year they met each other regularly in the course of their duties. They were both Masters of their livery companies (Tulse was a Grocer), merchants with the East India Company and the Royal African Company, Presidents of Bridewell and Bethlem Hospitals and Lord Mayors – at different times. They suffered the insult of being dismissed as Aldermen by King James II in 1687, returning to office together in 1688. Finally, Geffery and Tulse were buried in the same church.

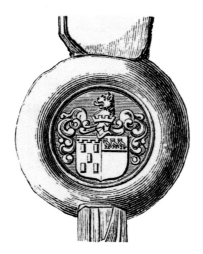

PREVIOUS PAGE
Sir Robert Geffery's coat of arms was registered with the College of Arms a month after he had been knighted in 1673. The six 'billets' (small bars of iron or steel) referred to his connection with the Ironmongers' Company

LEFT
Geffery's seal, attached to a document of 1658. He incorporated three owls from the arms of the Cropley family following his marriage to Priscilla Cropley in 1651

SHERIFF

The ceremony of presenting the Sheriffs of London at the Court of Exchequer, Palace of Westminster. C.J.M. Wichelo, 1811. The figure centre foreground is the back view of the presiding official

Geffery's election to the office of Sheriff was received enthusiastically by his fellow Ironmongers, for in the normal course of events he would advance from Sheriff to Alderman and ultimately to the mayoralty, bringing prestige to his Company, which had not boasted a Lord Mayor since 1635–6. In preparation for the river procession to the Palace of Westminster, where Geffery swore the oath of office on Lord Mayor's Day 1673, the Ironmongers' ceremonial barge, built three years ago, was overhauled, and liverymen of the Company looked forward to the prospect of a celebratory dinner. So began a year of arduous duties for Geffery (carried out with the assistance of the Sheriff's yeoman, who lived in Geffery's house), and lavish entertaining at considerable personal expense (Sir Dudley North spent £2,000 during his shrieval year, 1682–3, the equivalent of some £260,000 at 2012 values).[4] In view of his forthcoming expenses, Geffery was delighted to accept a subsidy from the Ironmongers' Company, which voted him 100 nobles 'towards the trimming of his house' (a noble was originally a gold coin worth 6 shillings 8 pence). Nor did he hesitate to request the loan of

95

the Ironmongers' best gold and silver cups, 200 silver flagons, basins, tankards, bowls and three dozen gilt spoons valued at £1,291.[5] This valuable haul was delivered to Geffery's house in time for the dinner he hosted on 18 November for sixty-four liverymen of the Ironmongers' Company who were joined by his neighbour and fellow Churchwarden, Philip Jackson, and two former apprentices, John Silverlocke and William Pendarris.

As soon as he received his knighthood from King Charles II in October 1673, Sir Robert Geffery was in touch with Sir Edward Bysshe FRS, Clarenceux King of Arms at the College of Arms. Somewhat impudently, Geffery had awarded himself an unauthorised coat of arms soon after his marriage to Priscilla Cropley in 1651 (her family were landed gentry), incorporating three owls from the Cropley arms and five billets (small bars of iron or steel). Once he was knighted, Geffery registered his arms formally with the College, whereupon the Cropley reference was dropped and Geffery's connections with the Ironmongers' Company were reinforced by 'six billets sable'.[6]

As a contemporary pamphlet stressed, 'the office of a sheriff of London, is of all others, a trust of the greatest weight and importance. For besides their having the power over the posse of London and Middlesex, and the right of returning juries both in capital and civil causes, not only all offenders but all debtors are committed to their custody'.[7] Geffery's duties were now magisterial. He possessed the power to arrest, to serve the King's writs and compel men to obey the law; prisoners in the City gaols, debtors and the disorderly were under his charge and in fulfilling his duties at the Sheriff's Court, Geffery gained a reputation as an excellent magistrate. Furthermore, during his term of office he promoted reforms to the City's finances, putting his name to *A Report on the General State of the Chamber Accounts for the City of London* (1674).

The office of Sheriff brought Geffery into direct contact with Charles II, as for example, when the Court of Aldermen instructed Geffery and Tulse to attend the King to plead against the impressment of seamen aboard the ship *Elizabeth* which had been destined for Newcastle to load coal for the City. The Sheriffs' case was for the release of the men and the ship because the inhabitants of London were in desperate need of fuel during the winter of 1673–4.[8] England was at war with the Dutch, hence the King required sailors for his fleet, but as far as the Aldermen and Sheriffs were concerned, coal for the inhabitants of London was a priority.

As Sheriff, Geffery became acquainted with an ambitious young lawyer, George Jeffreys (1645–89), the Common Serjeant of London, who was to become notorious for his conduct of the 'Bloody Assizes' in the west of England (see pages 121, 132–3). When the two men first met, Geffery was regularly at Guildhall to confer with Jeffreys on legal matters. He was some thirty years older than Jeffreys,

OPPOSITE
Guildhall and Guildhall Yard, looking north. Published by Johannes de Ram, *c.*1700

The South Prospect of GUILD HALL

yet they formed a longstanding friendship based on loyalty to the monarch and debauched dinners. It was said that at the start of his career, Jeffreys cultivated attorneys and City dignitaries such as Sir Robert Clayton and Sir Robert Geffery, 'which probably inclined him [Jeffreys] to steer his course that way; where, having got acquaintance with the city attorneys and drinking desperately with them he came into full business and was chosen Recorder of the City', in 1678.[9] Geffery and Jeffreys mixed in the same circles, were drinking companions and in the year that Geffery was Lord Mayor, Jeffreys was Lord Chancellor. Disgraced and arrested in 1688 when he tried to leave the country, Lord Chancellor Jeffreys was comforted in his hour of need by Geffery (see page 151).

The dignity and magisterial duties of Sheriff suited Geffery. He seemed to relish the status and privileges of office, the ceremonies and entertainments. He was a familiar figure at City dinners, he frequented coffee-houses and The Mitre Tavern, lived in a large mansion and kept a coach and horses. Sociable, ambitious, an astute merchant and a practical businessman with civic and political interests, Geffery had no inclination for intellectual or artistic activities: the flowering of the arts and sciences during the reign of King Charles II passed him by, although he knew Christopher Wren, Robert Hooke, Samuel Pepys, Edward Tyson and other Fellows of the Royal Society. As Deputy of his Ward, he was probably among the 'chief Aldermen and Magistrates' who entertained Fellows of the Royal Society to a 'Collation to welcome us to our first place of Assembly' (Gresham College) in December 1674.[10] A 'collation' in the company of Fellows, Aldermen and Deputies would have appealed to Geffery, but the scientific and sometimes eccentric pursuits of the Royal Society were not to his taste. Nor is there any evidence of his patronage of the arts or literary pursuits; he was neither a theatre-goer like Pepys nor a scholar like Evelyn. After his death in 1704, bundles of banknotes were found at his house, also plate, jewels, merchandise and household items to the value of £408; there is no mention of a library, paintings, tapestries or important pieces of furniture, either in his will or his executors' accounts.[11] Geffery was blessed with a strong Christian faith, good judgement and financial acumen; he devoted time to the City's charities and had a soft spot for the welfare of children. He was forthright in manner and speech, totally trustworthy and he commanded respect. These down-to-earth qualities were laced with social aspirations, and his portrait by Sir Godfrey Kneller suggests there was an element of vanity about Geffery. His stance in front of the presidential throne, the elaborate wig and the inclusion of the mayoral chain with the sword of state, several years after he had been Lord Mayor, reflect pride, if not vanity. The display of mayoral insignia was not unusual: other mayoral portraits of the same era featured the trappings of office, for example Da Castro's painting of a grim Sir Robert Clayton (c.1680), Gerard Soest's portrayal of a lugubrious Sir Joseph Sheldon (1678) and Mary Beale's sober Sir William Turner (1675) – but none of those sitters convey the monarchic swagger of Sir Robert Geffery.

'THE BURNING OF THE WHORE OF BABYLON'

Sir Robert Geffery's year as Sheriff commenced with a baptism by fire. A week after he had been sworn in, he faced a potentially dangerous situation. Since the discovery of the Gunpowder Plot on 5 November 1605, the anniversary had been celebrated as 'the day of deliverance of our Church and State from the hellish

Powder-plot'.[12] Henceforward, the arrest and execution of the Catholic conspirators associated with Guy Fawkes was marked by bonfires, and in November 1673 an outburst of anti-catholicism gave vent to uproarious anti-popery demonstrations by Londoners who particularly objected to the recent marriage of the Catholic Duke of York to Mary of Modena, an Italian. Hundreds of bonfires lit the streets and fireworks flew 'like Bees through the Ayre'. The apprentices made an effigy of the Pope, 'the whore of Babylon' as they called him, which was carried in a torchlight procession of more than 1,000 people to the Poultry market

OPPOSITE
Detail from Ogilby and
Morgan's map of 1676
showing the Honourable
Artillery Company's
Ground, with four
regiments of pikemen
and musketeers drawn
up in battle formation

place. The effigy was suspended on a rope from garret windows across Poultry Street and a fire underneath it burned for twenty hours. Some let fly with pistols and 'fowling peices' (light-weight guns) to shoot 'the Pope' but before long, having 'filled themselves with good liquor', they departed. Violence was close to the surface but the demonstration subsided peacefully, absolving the Sheriffs from taking punitive measures. It was soon followed by another of the City's annual celebrations, held to mark the anniversary of Queen Elizabeth I's accession to the throne on 17 November 1558. This was another excuse for bonfires and 'pope-bashing' in the City, with pageants featuring Jesuits, monks and the despised trappings of catholicism carried in procession from the Green Yard, behind Geffery's house in Lime Street, to be burned joyfully at Temple Bar.

Not only the mob (the word, which derived from *mobile vulgus*, meaning the fickle crowd or rabble, came into use at this time), but also aristocrats, politicians and poets objected to the catholicism of the King's Court. The poet Andrew Marvell risked prosecution when in 1677 he alleged there existed a longstanding plan 'to change the Lawful Government of England into an Absolute Tyranny and to Convert the Established Protestant Religion into down-right Popery'.[13] The threat of 'down-right Popery' became a reality during the reign of James II, when the rulers of the City – Geffery as Lord Mayor (1685–6) and his allies, Alderman Sir William Pritchard (Lord Mayor 1682–3), Alderman Sir Peter Rich (a merchant and gunpowder manufacturer), and Alderman Sir William Russell (one of Geffery's executors) – had to deal with the riotous reaction to the King's policies, in particular, with the violent opposition to Catholic 'mass-houses' (see pages 136–40).

THE HONOURABLE ARTILLERY COMPANY

As he ascended the City hierarchy, Geffery made his mark at the Honourable Artillery Company, the oldest regiment of the British army, based in Finsbury then as now. Geffery signed the HAC's historic document known as the 'Ancient Vellum Book' on 17 August 1669,[14] along with Samuel Pepys, Sir Robert Clayton, Sir Thomas St George who was Garter King-at-Arms, Henry Howard, later Earl of Norwich and Marshal of England, Matthew Wren, who was Secretary to the Duke of York, *et al*. Although he was not yet a Sheriff, Geffery was already a well-known figure in the City, and was now launched in the superior social circles of the HAC. Four years later, in the year that he was chosen Sheriff and knighted by the King, Geffery was one of eight 'worthy persons' (with his friends Tulse, Pritchard and Smyth, among others) chosen to be Stewards for the HAC's forthcoming feast, which was attended by the Lord Mayor, Aldermen and

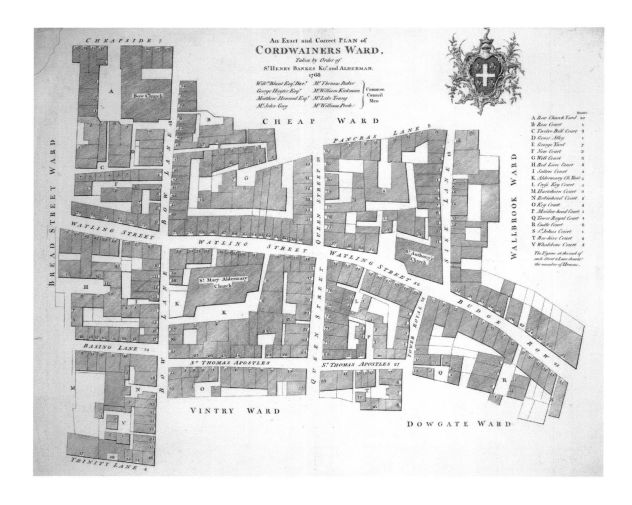

An Exact and Correct PLAN of
CORDWAINERS WARD.
Taken by Order of
Sr HENRY BANKES Knt. and ALDERMAN.
1768

Willm Blunt Esqr Depy	Mr Thomas Baker
George Hayter Esqr	Mr William Kirkman
Matthew Howard Esqr	Mr Luke Young
Mr John Gay	Mr William Peck

Common Council Men

CHEAP WARD

References

		Houses
A	Bow Church Yard	10
B	Rose Court	6
C	Twelve Bell Court	8
D	Goose Alley	1
E	George Yard	7
F	New Court	6
G	Well Court	8
H	Red Lion Court	9
I	Salters Court	9
K	Aldermary Ch. Yard	4
L	Cross Key Court	4
M	Hartshorn Court	0
N	Robinhood Court	2
O	Key Court	2
P	Maiden head Court	3
Q	Tower Royal Court	4
R	Castle Court	6
S	St Johns Court	1
T	Bee-hive Court	2
V	Whalebone Court	3

The Figures at the end of each Street & Lane denote the number of Houses.

CHEAPSIDE 7 · Bow Church · BREAD STREET WARD · WATLING STREET · BOW LANE · PANCRAS LANE 8 · QUEEN STREET · WALLBROOK WARD · WATLING STREET · St Mary Aldermary Church · St Anthony's Church · SISE LANE · BUDGE ROW · BASING LANE 12 · TOWER ROYAL · St THOMAS APOSTLES · St THOMAS APOSTLES 27 · QUEEN STREET · TRINITY LANE 4 · VINTRY WARD · DOWGATE WARD

---

aristocrats, and held at Merchant Taylors' Hall in 1674.[15] To be chosen Steward was an honour Geffery would have appreciated, and at the HAC's annual church service and feast for 1674 he was distinguished by the gilded staff he carried (the Stewards' emblem of office).

The choice of Geffery, Tulse, Pritchard and Smyth as Stewards steadied a volatile situation, for the previous year the HAC feast had been mired by scandal. Alderman Patience Ward, a plain-speaking Yorkshire Puritan who was to be Lord Mayor in 1680–1, and three other Aldermen (John Forth, Sir John Moore and Sir Francis Chaplin) had been chosen Stewards but, as Sir John Robinson, Lieutenant of the Tower of London put it in a letter to Sir Joseph Williamson, Ward and his confederates 'hung an asse and would not have any entertainment this year. Four commoners were chosen in their room'.[16] The Aldermen's refusal

Plan of Cordwainer Ward by William Chamberlaine, engraving by James Kirk, 1768. Geffery was Alderman of the Ward, 1676–1704

to act as Stewards was a protest against the Duke of York, Captain General of the HAC and heir to the throne, whose recent marriage to Mary of Modena held the dreaded prospect of a succession of Catholic monarchs. Again, when the Duke was invited to the feast in 1679, hundreds of his detractors sold or tore up their dinner tickets to demonstrate their opposition (1679 marked the start of the exclusion crisis which centred on legislation to prevent the Duke's accession to the throne). A portrait of the Duke of York, which hung at Guildhall, was mutilated early in 1682, and later that year his opponents in the HAC organised an alternative feast at Haberdashers' Hall so as to avoid dining in his presence. King Charles II brought the Company to heel by suspending its annual elections between 1681 and 1685, and when the Duke of York acceded to the throne as King James II, he had his revenge by cancelling the HAC's feast.

Honorary membership of the HAC gave Geffery prestige and access to an influential network of contacts; he was still taking part in the Company's activities at the age of eighty-seven, when he commanded the battalion in an exercise at arms (see page 155). Geffery's military connections were reinforced when he was appointed a Colonel of the Trained Bands by Charles II in April 1681. The King, being head of the militia, 'turned out' and 'putt in' whomsoever he pleased,[17] replacing those he did not trust with his chief adherents, such as Sir Robert Geffery and Chief Justice George Jeffreys. Four years later, in 1685, the two friends, now Lord Mayor Sir Robert Geffery and Lord Chancellor George Jeffreys, were commissioned to the Lieutenancy of the City of London. With Sir William Russell, John Jeffreys and Sir Peter Rich, they were the monarch's chief representatives and peacekeepers in the City.[18]

ALDERMAN OF CORDWAINER WARD

At midsummer 1676 Sir Robert Geffery was put forward by Sir John Sheldon (the current Lord Mayor), Sir William Turner (Lord Mayor 1668–9) and Sir John Shorter (Lord Mayor 1687–8), to be Alderman of Cordwainer Ward in succession to Sir Robert Clayton, the Whig banker who was to be Lord Mayor in 1679. Geffery's election was a vote of confidence from his peers, and held the prospect of the mayoralty. Aldermen of the City needed resources of some £10,000 for eligibility (the equivalent of some £1,250,000 at 2012 values),[19] and further financial resources were required on succession as Lord Mayor. Clearly, by 1676 Geffery was a merchant and civic leader of substance, wealth and renown.

Cordwainer Street Ward, as it was also known, was originally associated with cordwainers (makers of shoes and soft leather goods), curriers, hosiers and wealthy pepperers. The Ward boasted three churches: St Mary-le-Bow at the junction of Bow Lane with Cheapside, the ancient foundation of St Mary, Aldermary, at the south end of Bow Lane, and St Antholin on the corner of Watling Street and Budge Row, where dealers in budge (lambskin) used to live. All three churches had been destroyed or damaged in the Great Fire of 1666 and were being rebuilt to designs by Sir Christopher Wren while Geffery was Alderman of the Ward. This populous Ward was represented by eight Common Councillors (as compared to Lime Street Ward with four) and, apart from 1687–8 when he was one of the victims of King James II's cursory dismissals, Geffery fulfilled the office of Alderman of the Ward from 1676 until his death in 1704.

Geffery's first year as Alderman began tragically: his wife Priscilla died aged forty-two on 26 October 1676, after twenty-five years of marriage, leaving Geffery a sixty-three-year-old widower. Little is known about Priscilla – at the age of eighteen she had married a man twenty years her senior and, as Geffery's career advanced, she stood in his shadow. Priscilla left no will, no children, nor is the cause of her death recorded: there were numerous fevers, diseases, epidemics and afflictions that were often fatal, and surgery brought the added risk of infection. Dame Priscilla was buried in the chancel close to her husband's pew at their parish church, St Dionis, on 2 November.[20] The widower did not mourn for long: Alderman Geffery's strong sense of duty impelled him to work, so on 17 November he appeared at the Court of Aldermen to assist with the government of the City, especially with regard to the regulation of the markets – the Woolchurch or Stocks Market, Leadenhall and the meat markets at Newgate and Honey Lane – which were being surveyed by William Leybourn.

At meetings of the Court of Aldermen, the august tribunal that was the apogee of the City's government, Geffery was loaded with responsibilities from which he did not flinch. The Court dated from 1200 when 'five and twenty of the more discreet men of the City were sworn to take counsel on behalf of the City, together with the Mayor'.[21] It met in the Aldermen's court room at Guildhall and dealt with every aspect of City life, from matters of state to orphans. Geffery was soon heavily involved: he advised the wealthy Bridge House Estates and backed proposals for fire insurance for houses in the City; he was called upon to be an arbitrator at the Court of Requests, which heard cases for the recovery of small debts; he attended trials at Guildhall, advised the Court of Orphans and sat on committees of Common Council. He was concerned with the conservancy of the Thames (surveying the river, mending its banks and steps, removing obstructions such as rotten boats and entrails deposited by butchers) and of course he oversaw the governance and policing of his own Ward. Geffery's work for the Court of Orphans, which was responsible for orphans of freemen of the City, was the most time-consuming, heart-rending process. The personal

OPPOSITE
King Charles II painted
by John Michael Wright,
c.1660–65

circumstances of each orphan had to be carefully considered: the fair settlement of inheritances, apprenticeships and marriages had to be decided in the best interests of the child, as for example, 'the disposal the best they can of James, one of the sons and orphans of Jno Robinson, deceased, according to his father's desire'.[22]

THE KING AND THE CITY

The last decade of King Charles II's reign was punctuated by plots and rumours of plots that surfaced from the rising undercurrent of anti-catholicism. From the Popish Plot revealed by Titus Oates in 1678 to the Rye House Plot of 1683, fears for the King's safety tended to generate public sympathy for Charles, temporarily. In March 1679 relations between the King and the City of London were reported to be good, according to the Dowager Countess of Sunderland: 'His Majesty and his City of London are upon very good terms', she wrote. The King dined with the Lord Mayor and 'the people showed as much affection and duty as the expressions of such a time could be'. As for the Aldermen — Geffery and his companions — 'they drank the King's health over and over upon their knees and wished all hanged and damned that would not serve him as with their lives and fortunes'. It was not until 2 o'clock in the morning that the party adjourned and that was not the end of it. The Aldermen then escorted the King to Whitehall Palace, but 'would not trust him with his guards who were all drunks, but brought some of their own; and they all went merry out of the king's cellar'.[23] Later that year, when the King was suffering from the ague (an acute fever with paroxysms and sweating), the Aldermen were still dancing attendance by visiting him daily, whatever their motives.

Bonhomie between King Charles II, the House of Commons and the elders of the City of London was superficial. Relations had been deteriorating since at least 1673; the Court party was defeated in the general election of February 1679, and the unpopularity of the Catholic Duke of York forced him to go into temporary exile. The appalling prospect of the Duke's accession to the throne prompted a Bill in Parliament to exclude him from the succession: this was defeated by the House of Lords, narrowly and after violent clashes. With the accession of a Roman Catholic King looming, anti-catholicism permeated the country, stirring Protestant superstition, inspiring pamphlets and sermons and prompting an attempt to assassinate both Charles and his brother, James, Duke of York, in 1683.

Gilbert Burnet (1643–1715, later Bishop of Salisbury) expressed the views of many of the King's subjects when he preached at St Mary-le-Bow in 1680. Gloriously rebuilt by Wren, the church was the pride of Cordwainer Ward and, as Alderman of the Ward, Geffery was in a prominent position at the service held there on 2 September, to mark the anniversary fast held in memory of the Great Fire that had destroyed this church and over eighty others. To an appreciative audience led by the Lord Mayor, Sir Robert Clayton, and some two dozen Aldermen, Burnet celebrated 'the great Splendor of London rebuilt', moving swiftly on to warn of 'the worst Effects of Popery' and the danger of being 'secretly corrupted with some of the worst Principles of that Religion'. Burnet was a powerful preacher, not afraid to scold the King and give voice to anti-catholicism, and in this sermon he stressed that the Anglican Church was 'the greatest Bulwark against Popery'. The Lord Mayor and Aldermen expressed their approval by ordering the publication of Burnet's sermon.[24] A few months later, Burnet preached on the same theme to the House of Commons and consequently found himself dismissed from his lectureship at St Clement Danes by order of the King.

WHIGS AND TORIES

As religious issues between the monarch and his subjects hardened, the City became a hot-bed of party politics. The Whigs opposed the succession to the throne of James, Duke of York, because he was a Roman Catholic, and the Tories, loyal to the monarchy, opposed his exclusion. The words Whig and Tory were originally insults, Whigs being named after Presbyterian rebels who had marched through Edinburgh in 1648, while Tories referred to Irish outlaws who plundered and killed English Protestants. During the reign of Charles II the loyalists who came to be called Tories were ranged behind the Earl of Ailesbury (a gentleman of the bedchamber to the King). This was no mere dining club, but an alliance of some 300 of the nobility, Privy Councillors, militia officers, courtiers, the Recorder of London and the majority of Aldermen – Geffery must have been among them – who were devoted to the King and the Church of England and who met at The Warder, Ludgate, from 1681.[25]

Opposing this party were the Whigs of the Green Ribbon Club, led by Sir Thomas Player. They gathered at the King's Head Tavern in Fleet Street from 1674, sporting green ribbons in their hats. In the vituperative shrieval elections of June 1682, Thomas Papillon, a Mercer, auditor for the City Corporation and intermittent MP for Dover, and John Dubois, deacon of the French Church in Threadneedle Street, represented the Whigs, while Sir Peter Rich and Sir Dudley North stood for the Tory party. When the majority of votes went to the two Whigs, Papillon and Dubois, the King ordered new elections to ensure that the City was governed by his supporters, beginning with the installation of the two Tory Sheriffs, Rich and North.

After losing the City elections of 1682, the Whigs fell into disarray and were discredited by their association with the Rye House Plot to assassinate the King in 1683. During this era of duplicity, suspicion and plots, measures were enforced to seek out papists, nonconformists and all conspirators, whatever their politics. Supporters of the Duke of Monmouth's rebellion were organising bases at dissenters' meeting houses and Robert Geffery and Henry Tulse were among seven magistrates issued with warrants to break up these 'seditious conventicles', by force if necessary, and to take into custody the preachers and their followers. Geffery was responsible for investigating dissenters' meetings at Mugwell Street, St Paul's Alley, Plaisterers' Hall and Glovers' Hall.[26] The disbursement of meetings was difficult; congregations melted away and re-formed elsewhere and even the official policy wavered.

ALDERMEN ARRESTED

Following the imposition of Tory Sheriffs in the hotly disputed and legally dubious elections of 1682, Papillon and Dubois took out a writ against the current Lord Mayor, Sir William Pritchard, and the Aldermen Sir John Moore (who had been Lord Mayor during the crisis of June 1682), Sir Henry Tulse (Lord Mayor 1683–4), Sir James Smyth (who was to be Lord Mayor in 1684) and Robert Geffery, who was also in line to be Lord Mayor. Two Whig attorneys, Gilbert Nelson and Richard Goodenough, acted on behalf of Papillion and Dubois and in carrying out the writ, Nelson and the City Coroner, John Brome, took the radical decision to arrest the Lord Mayor and 'divers Aldermen of this City'.[27] This provoked violence: 'disorderly people' gathered with staves and clubs, swords were drawn and the City Marshal threatened to slit the Coroner's brains. Geffery was among the Tory Aldermen rounded-up by Coroner Brome and he was later called upon to give evidence relating to the dramatic proceedings of 24–25 April 1683. As it happened, Tulse provided the evidence, so Geffery was not called upon. However, in his affidavit, Gilbert Nelson claimed that Smyth and Geffery had insulted him, 'gave him very reviling words, calling him rogue and the like', and that Smyth had incited the Lord Mayor to commit Nelson to Newgate Prison.[28]

The Court of Aldermen reacted grimly to the arrest of the Lord Mayor and several Aldermen, which was condemned as 'an Act of unparalleled insolence and high affront to ye good men of this City'. A committee was nominated 'to consider what is fit to be done hereupon for intimidating ye honour of his Lordship and the government of this City'.[29] The affront to the Lord Mayor, the Aldermen and the dignity of the City was indeed pursued, with the intention of

OPPOSITE
Portrait of Thomas
Papillon by Sir Godfrey
Kneller, 1698

'discountenancing and punishing the authors of the said Act'.[30] In the face of such formidable opposition, Papillon and Dubois dropped their case. However Pritchard, Geffery and their party took the matter through the courts doggedly, claiming false arrest. They triumphed: Pritchard was awarded £10,000 in damages from Papillon, who fled to Utrecht. Dubois died promptly; Nelson left the country and Goodenough went underground as evidence surfaced that he and his gang of conspirators had planned to secure control of the City, murder the Lord Mayor and the entire Court of Aldermen, then 'hang their skins at Guildhall'.[31]

THE STUARTS' REVENGE

The imposition of Tory Sheriffs in the City elections of 1682 was the prelude to an exercise of the royal prerogative by King Charles II which brought the City and its livery companies under his control. The *Quo Warranto* proceedings launched by the King in 1683 questioned by what authority the City wielded its power and independence, its legality and privileges. During this enquiry, which lasted until 1688, the City was forced to surrender its independence to the King, who picked the Lord Mayor, Aldermen, Sheriffs, City officials and liverymen by name. By this and similar means 'the proudest corporation in the world was at the feet of a Stuart'.[32]

A writ of *Quo Warranto* was received by the Ironmongers' Company early in 1684 when it was laid before the Master, Captain William Walker, and the Court of Assistants for discussion. On behalf of the Company, a petition was drafted for delivery to the King at Windsor in April. Sir Robert Geffery 'upon his knees', accompanied by the two Wardens likewise in obeisance, presented a sycophantic plea for pardon to the King. Geffery pointed out that the Ironmongers' Company dated its incorporation to 1463, its legality and privileges had been confirmed by successive charters, yet 'for reasons best known unto Your Majesty', a writ of *Quo Warranto* 'hath been brought against your petitioners by which they are deeply sensible of Your Majesty's displeasure'.[33] A further plea was made by a deputation of Ironmongers who arranged to meet the Attorney General at The Bull's Head in Fleet Street to present their case, to no avail. Submission was imperative; in common with the other livery companies, the Ironmongers could only bow to the King's will.

So the City of London and its livery companies were subjected to King Charles II's authority, indefinitely. This blow from the absolutist monarch questioned the legality and status not only of the City of London and its livery companies but also of corporations throughout the kingdom.

THE GREAT FROST

As the relentless process of *Quo Warranto* was implemented, London suffered a cruel winter, possibly the most severe in its history. 'The Great Frost' of 1683–4 lasted thirteen weeks and brought intense hardship to the inhabitants of London. Trees split and cattle, birds, fish, plants and crops perished of the cold. There was no water in the pipes, the frozen Thames locked ships in ice and there was a shortage of fuel. Despite the harsh conditions, there was fun to be had on the river, which supported 'a Continual Faire' between Westminster and The Temple. People slid across the ice on sledges and skates – even coaches trundled over the thick layer of ice. Although wood, coal and corn were scarce, entertainment was in good supply in the form of bull-baiting, horse and coach races, puppet plays, interludes and tippling, 'so it all seemed to be a baccanalia'.[34]

In Geffery's parish, St Dionis, the shortage of fuel was alleviated by the distribution of 200 faggots of wood to the poor, the gift of Sir Henry Tulse, the Lord Mayor. Shortly before the onset of this exceptionally harsh winter, liverymen of the Ironmongers' Company had celebrated Tulse's inauguration on Lord Mayor's Day, 29 October 1683, participating in the river procession and marching in procession through the City streets. As an Alderman, Geffery had a seat on the City's barge where he was well-placed to watch the formalities closely – for him this was a rehearsal for his own Lord Mayor's Day two years later.

Lord Mayor elect

When the City resumed its sober countenance in the spring of 1684, the surrender of charters by the livery companies was in full flow. The Ironmongers' fifteenth-century document was submitted to the King in July by Geffery, leading the deputation: being an Alderman and Lord Mayor elect he was his Company's representative at Court and in the City. The Ironmongers' Company also looked to Geffery to take the lead to prevent it from 'sinking' because of the lack of apprentices coming forward.[35] This was attributed to competition from the Tin Plate Workers', the Pattenmakers' (pattens were wooden shoes mounted on an iron ring), the Needle and Pin Makers', Innholders' and Brewers' Companies. Apprenticeships with these relatively new companies were cheaper and possibly less restrictive than apprenticeships with one of the 'Great Twelve'. It is unlikely that Geffery could have rectified the situation, although his personal reputation and imminent election as Lord Mayor would have enhanced his Company's status vis-à-vis the lesser companies.

Polychrome plaster model for a statue of King Edward IV for the Royal Exchange, attributed to Caius Gabriel Cibber, 1684–5. Edward IV granted the Ironmongers' Company its charter of incorporation in 1463

FOLLOWING PAGES
A Frost Fair on the Thames at Temple Stairs, during the winter of 1683–4. Oil painting by Abraham Hondius, 1684

With a seat on the Court of Aldermen, Geffery could and did promote the Ironmongers' bid to erect a statue of King Edward IV at the new Royal Exchange. Nicholas Leate, Master of the Ironmongers' Company three times in the early seventeenth century, had in 1610 initiated the project to adorn the Royal Exchange with statues of the kings and queens of England. With the building of the second Royal Exchange after the Great Fire, the Lord Mayor issued a precept to the livery companies encouraging them to set up new statues to replace those that had perished. There was rivalry between the Ironmongers, the Tallow Chandlers and the Barber Surgeons, who competed to sponsor a statue of King Edward IV for one of the niches in the quadrangle of the Exchange. All three companies claimed Edward IV as their founder (he had granted the Ironmongers' charter of incorporation in 1463) and were eager to stress their historic origins and their allegiance to the monarchy. As the most prestigious company of the three, a connection with the originator of the scheme and with Geffery as an influential protagonist, the Ironmongers' Company won the bid. Geffery's assistance in procuring the desired outcome was duly acknowledged, and the statue of Edward IV was commissioned from the mason Thomas Cartwright, who was known to Geffery for his work at St Mary-le-Bow.[36] Following a fire at the Royal Exchange in January 1838, the Ironmongers' Company requested the return of the statue, but it had either been destroyed by the fire or auctioned and has not been seen since.

In January 1685 the Master of the Ironmongers, Captain William Walker, and Sir Robert Geffery dined with The Rt Hon. the Lord Mayor, Sir James Smyth, who had been Geffery's ally during the scandalous arrests of Aldermen in 1683. In February King Charles II died, having been received into the Church of Rome on his deathbed. The accession of his brother as King James II unleashed a series of events that affected Walker and Geffery personally. Within the year, Walker was dismissed in favour of Geffery, who was appointed Master of the Ironmongers' Company and Lord Mayor of London by royal command.

Endnotes

1 The word sheriff derives from shire reeve, the local official holding jurisdiction under the king **2** A.B. Beaven, *The Aldermen of the City of London* (1908–13), vol II, p.188 **3** SPD, 3 October 1673, pp.557, 566 **4** Figures derived from E.H. Phelps Brown and Sheila V. Hopkins, 'Seven centuries of the prices of consumables compared with builders' wage rates', *Economica*, November 1956, and the UK Retail Price Index 2012, www.wolfbane.com/rpi **5** CMIC, 29 October, 11 November 1673, GL MS. 16967/6 **6** Geffery's arms were registered with the College of Arms on 24 November 1673, Misc. Grants 2/20 and Misc. Grants 6 ff.60v–61r. See also Add. MS. 5533, f.242/129, BL, and Nicholl p.569, and Appendix xx, p.XLVI, and John Nicholl, *Miscellanea genealogica et heraldica* (1868), vol I, p.328 **7** Anon, *The rights of the city farther unfolded… in relation to the present action of sheriffs* (1682), p.1 **8** 13 January 1674, Rep 79 **9** Roger North, *The Lives of the Norths*, ed. A. Jessopp (1890), vol I, p.273 **10** JE, vol IV, 1 December 1674, p.27. The City authorities had overseen the rebuilding of London after the Great Fire from Gresham College, situated between Bishopsgate and Broad Street **11** Geffery's will, 10 February 1704, PRO/PROB11/475, and Executors' Accounts, 1707, C9/332/55, TNA **12** *The Burning of the Whore of Babylon. As it was Acted, with great Applause, in the Poultrey, London, on Wednesday night, being the fifth of November at 6 of the o'clock* (1673), pp.3–4 **13** Andrew Marvell, *An Account of the Growth of Popery and Arbitrary Government in England* (1677), p.69 **14** Geffery's signature in the 'Ancient Vellum Book' seems to mark the start of his association with the HAC, although the date may be inaccurate. He was appointed Steward for the 1674 feast on 9 October 1673. Pepys was a Steward in 1677 **15** G.A. Raikes, *The Ancient Vellum Book of the Honourable Artillery Company* (1890), pp.7, 8, 125 **16** SPD, 24 October 1673, pp.594–5. 'To hang an arse/asse' meant to hang back. Forth and Moore were nonconformists; Pepys described Chaplin as outspoken **17** Narcissus Luttrell, *A Brief Historical Relation of State Affairs from September 1678 to April 1714* (1857), rev. edn. 1969, vol I, p.76 **18** SPD, February 1685, pp.56, 86 **19** See note 4 **20** *Registers of St Dionis London 1538–1754*, Harleian Society (1878), vol 3, p.243 **21** Ben Weinreb, C. Hibbert, Julia Keay, John Keay, *The London Encyclopaedia* (2008), p.13 **22** 27 February 1683, Rep 88 **23** Henry Sidney, *Diary of the Times of Charles II* (1843), vol I, pp.301–2 **24** Gilbert Burnet, *A Sermon Preached before the Rt Hon the Lord Mayor and Aldermen of the City of London at Bow Church, 2 September 1680* (1681) **25** Another Tory club met at Fullers Rents from 1679 to 1684 **26** James P. Malcolm, *Anecdotes of the Manners and Customs of the City of London from the Roman Invasion to the year 1700* (1811), vol II, p.83 **27** 26 April 1683, Rep 88 **28** SPD, April 1683, pp.204–6, 214–5 **29** 26 April 1683, Rep 88 **30** Ibid. **31** *A True Account and Declaration of the Late Horrid Conspiracy against the Late King*, published by the Earl of Sunderland (1685) **32** David Ogg, *England in the Reign of Charles II* (1962), vol II, p.639 **33** Nicholl, p.289 **34** JE, vol IV, 14, 24 January 1684, pp.361–2 **35** CMIC, 17 August 1682, GL MS. 16967/6 **36** Ibid., 5 November 1684, and Ironmongers' Company Wardens' Accounts, May 1685, GL MS. 16988/6. Cartwright subcontracted the work to Arnold Quellin, see Katharine Gibson, 'The Kingdom's Marble Chronicle', *The Royal Exchange*, ed. Ann Saunders (1997), especially p.161 and plate IVC

5 | THE RT HON. THE LORD MAYOR

King Charles II died early in February 1685 in communion with the Church of Rome. His brother James, Duke of York, whose conversion to catholicism had been confirmed by the Pope in 1676, was crowned on 23 April. To begin with, King James II was mindful to secure the support of Parliament and the City of London, both being vital to his purposes. His policy was blatantly successful, as Luttrell observed, 'great tricks and practices were used to bring in men affected to the King and to keep out all those they call whigs or trimmers'.[1] Thus it was that in March 1685 the Ironmongers' Company received a new charter from the King, 'to make our beloved Sir Robert Jeffrey knt *(sic)*, to be the first and present master'.[2] The Wardens and Assistants were likewise chosen by the King and they were all required to swear the oaths of allegiance and supremacy and to take communion at St Peter's, Cornhill.

King James's charter of March 1685 conferred to the Ironmongers the duty of government by a Master, Wardens and Court of Assistants, all of whom were the King's nominees. This contravened the Company's tradition of independent government by Quarterly Courts constituted by the Master, Wardens and liverymen. Resentful of the changes imposed upon them by the monarch, the Ironmongers reacted negatively: no more than eight or twelve Assistants attended Court meetings between 1685 and 1688. On the return to the Company of its surrender under the *Quo Warranto* proceedings (see page 110) and the grant of Letters Patent by King James on 19 November 1688 (threatened as he then was by Prince William of Orange who had landed at Torbay), the Company resumed its traditional custom of Quarterly Courts. Twenty-seven members, including Geffery, crowded into the court room for the meeting on 21 November, signifying their profound relief at the restoration of the *status quo*.

Meanwhile, the changes demanded by King James's charter of March 1685 incensed the incumbent Master of the Ironmongers' Company, Captain William Walker (1635–1708), who found himself dismissed in favour of 'our beloved Sir Robert Jeffrey'. Walker was a Whig (some of whom were associated with conspiracies against the Stuarts), hence his expulsion. When the Clerk of the Ironmongers called on Walker to demand the surrender of the Company's documents and seal for transferral to Geffery, Walker was defiant. No, he would not hand over the key of the box containing the seal and he refused to do so until his term as Master expired, which in the normal course of events was some months ahead. If the Company wanted its seal before then, Walker fumed, someone would have to break open the box.[3] Walker's indignation was understandable but lacked conviction because there were duplicate keys to the box. Nevertheless, he clung on to his key and in 1687 he was reinstated as Master by King James (he served for a third term, 1693–4). Despite the altercation over the keys, Walker, who was Deputy for Farringdon Ward Without, and Geffery, Alderman of Cordwainer Ward, campaigned together for a superior pew for the Ironmongers' Company in the new St Paul's Cathedral.[4]

As Master of the Ironmongers' Company at the King's command, Geffery found himself in an awkward position, being a devout member of the Church of England arbitrarily appointed by the Catholic monarch to replace Walker, his fellow Ironmonger. Twenty-two members of the Company refused to take the oaths of allegiance and supremacy to King James, so were reported to the Court of Aldermen, which must have been a further embarrassment to Geffery. He had no option but to accept his appointment as Master in accordance with the charter issued by the King in March, but he wisely deferred to the Company's tradition of confirming the Master for the forthcoming year in July. Thus at the Confirmation Court of 1685, Geffery, after only four months in office, was superseded by John Breedon. However, Breedon pleaded 'weakness and indisposition of body' and asked to be replaced, suggesting William Hinton as his substitute (like Geffery, Breedon and Hinton had been Masters some years previously).[5] In this juggling of personnel, four Masters presided over the Ironmongers in the space of one year – Walker, Geffery, Breedon and Hinton.

For the time being, Geffery was in favour at the Court of King James. A few months after he had been appointed Master of the Ironmongers' Company, the King nominated him Lord Mayor of London. As he had done on his election as Sheriff, Geffery requested the loan of the Ironmongers' best pieces of silverware so that he could entertain in style, beginning with a dinner for members of the Company (the Ironmongers' Court voted 40 guineas towards his expenses, for which Geffery returned 'hearty thanks').[6] It had been fifty years since the last Ironmonger Lord Mayor, so Geffery's elevation was celebrated extravagantly. An organising committee met in the convivial atmosphere of North's coffee-house near Guildhall, to make plans for Geffery's inauguration, beginning with the repair of the ceremonial barge and the commissioning of a carving of the Company's arms

PREVIOUS PAGE
King James II of England
and Ireland (James VII of
Scotland), by Sir Godfrey
Kneller. Painted in 1684,
the year before he acceded
to the throne

ABOVE
King James II's charter
to the Ironmongers'
Company, March 1685,
appointing 'our beloved
Sir Robert Jeffrey knt'
as Master

to adorn its stern. Musicians were alerted, the great streamer, ribbons and the Admiral's flag were unpacked (the Lord Mayor being Admiral of the port of London, was entitled to fly a white ensign crossed with the sword of St Paul), and four gallons of canary wine were ordered for consumption on the barge during the river journey to Westminster on a bleak October day. New gowns were made for liverymen of the Company and new banners were commissioned, depicting St Laurence, who had been martyred by being secured to a grid-iron and roasted by a fire beneath (AD 258). The gridiron provided a tenuous reference to the Ironmongers' trade, and the adoption of a patron saint was intended to endear the Company to Catholic King James: a carving of St Laurence, made for the barge in 1740, can be seen at the hall.

The pageantry of Lord Mayor's Day 1685 was the preface to a year that seethed with rumours of conspiracies, and in this respect Geffery was the King's informant in the City, reporting on anyone who posed a threat to the monarch. However, in the spring of 1686 he incurred the King's displeasure when he shut down a 'mass-house' in Lime Street in order to avoid anti-Catholic riots. While some of the King's ministers, including the Lord Chancellor, continued to support King James and his policies, Geffery's uncompromising loyalty to the Church of England and the City led to his dismissal as Alderman by the King in 1687.

OPPOSITE, FROM LEFT
Geffery/Jeffrey was
appointed Master of the
Ironmongers' Company
by royal command,
1685. A detail from King
James's charter

The carving of St
Laurence, patron saint
of the Ironmongers'
Company. The Company
first adopted St Laurence
for Geffery's mayoral
year, 1685. This pinewood
carving was made for the
Company's barge in 1740.
He carries a gridiron, on
which he is said to have
been roasted

RIGHT
The execution of the
Duke of Monmouth and
Buccleuch at Tower Hill,
15 July 1685

DUKE OF MONMOUTH'S REBELLION

The 9th Earl of Argyll (1629–85) returned to Scotland in May 1685 to lead a rebellion against King James II of England (who was also King James VII of Scotland). Argyll's force of 2,500 men was easily vanquished and Argyll was captured and executed without trial. In June a more serious threat appeared in the form of the Duke of Monmouth (1649–85), Charles II's illegitimate son and a Protestant, who landed at Lyme Regis with the aim of deposing King James. Monmouth's rebellion gained enthusiastic support in the south-west, where some 3,000 supporters were recruited. The rebels were soundly defeated at the battle of Sedgemoor in July and Lord Chief Justice George Jeffreys subsequently brought some 1,380 men to trial at the 'Bloody Assizes', condemning 250 or so to execution and 850 to transportation to the West Indies. In London, the Duke of Monmouth was marched to Tower Hill, 'where his head was severed from his body in five strokes and put into a red silk bag'.[7] The Monmouth rebellion failed and its perpetrators were punished, yet its ramifications were felt throughout the country: 'few days pass without someone or other being yet apprehended'.[8]

In the aftermath of Monmouth's rebellion, the atmosphere in the City of London was one of suspicion and retribution. Shortly before Geffery's inauguration as Lord Mayor, Alderman Henry Cornish was charged with treason for implication in a plot to murder King Charles II and the Duke of York at Rye House, near Hoddesdon, as they returned to London from Newmarket in 1683, and with aiding and abetting the Monmouth rebellion two years later. Cornish was found guilty; he was executed on 23 October 1685 for all to see at the corner of King Street and Cheapside, then his head was delivered to Guildhall. On the day after the river procession that celebrated Geffery's installation as Lord Mayor, two other rebels were put to death on grounds of treason: John Ayloffe was executed at Temple Gate and Richard Nelthorpe was hanged, drawn and quartered at Gray's Inn Gate. In December, Lord Brandon was executed, and Charles Batemen, surgeon to the Earl of Shaftesbury, was sentenced to death for conspiring to kill the late King – and so it went on, with the Lord Mayor, Sir Robert Geffery, responsible for hunting down and reporting conspirators in the City. Subsequent trials for treason were conducted by his ally, George Jeffreys, created Lord Chancellor, High Steward and Baron Jeffreys of Wem, on his return to London from the 'Bloody Assizes' in the west country, in September 1685.

'LONDON'S ANNUAL TRIUMPH'[9]

Monmouth's rebellion and the 'Bloody Assizes' of the summer of 1685 created tension throughout the country, but at Ironmongers' Hall the threat to national security was forgotten as the Company prepared to celebrate Sir Robert Geffery's Lord Mayor's Day. The organisation of the entertainments proceeded apace with the choice of Matthew Taubman as the poet for the pageants. Taubman had come to notice for his eulogy to James, Duke of York, on his return from Scotland in 1682, so he could be relied upon to flatter King James II, as he now was, the guest of honour at Geffery's mayoral dinner. This was Taubman's first pageant for a Lord Mayor of London and he did well, judging by the fact that he was commissioned to write the Lord Mayors' pageants for the next three years. The painter-stainer, Richard Wallis, was responsible for the banners and heraldic painting for Geffery's pageants and Charles Williams for the designs.

The day before the public celebrations, on the feast of St Simon and St Jude, a solemn ceremony took place at Guildhall, whereby the outgoing Lord Mayor, Sir James Smyth, transferred to Geffery the symbols of office – the gold and enamel mayoral collar or chain of office hung with its precious jewel, the sceptre, mace, sword, keys, purse and cap. Not a word was exchanged on this poignant occasion, known as The Silent Change, which remains one of the City's traditions. The

OPPOSITE
The Lord Mayor's sceptre, sword, cap of maintenance, mace, chain of office and a loving cup used at official dinners. The sword and chain of office can be seen in Kneller's portrait of Sir Robert Geffery (page 99). A late-seventeenth-century oil painting attributed to Pieter Gerritsz van Roestraten

FOLLOWING PAGES
The Lord Mayor's river procession from the City to Westminster, British school. The painting fits the description of the procession on 29 October 1683 when Sir Robert Geffery's friend, Sir Henry Tulse, was installed as Lord Mayor. Alderman Geffery would have been in the City's barge, second from right

next morning, Thursday 29 October, members of the Ironmongers' Company assembled at their hall in Fenchurch Street at 7 o'clock, forming the nucleus of a procession that was led by sixty poor men who received charity from the Company. They were given new caps to wear, standards or banners to carry and supplied with bread, cheese and strong beer for breakfast. The procession was kept in order by fifty gentlemen ushers sporting velvet coats, gold chains and bearing white staves. Ranks of bachelors in their hooded gowns preceded the liverymen, weighed down by their voluminous fur-trimmed robes, followed by the Masters and Wardens of other companies in their regalia, escorted by standard bearers, thirty-six trumpeters, pipes and drums. The City Marshals attended on horseback, with a Master of Defence, and when all were assembled, the cavalcade moved off to Grocers' Hall to escort Sir James Smyth and the Aldermen to Guildhall, where they were joined by Sir Robert Geffery.

At Three Cranes Wharf, the elaborately decorated barges were moored, poised to row Geffery, the Aldermen, liverymen of the Ironmongers' Company and representatives of other senior livery companies to Westminster, where Geffery swore the oath 'to be true and faithful to His Majesty and Government', in the presence of the Lords and Barons of the Exchequer. The river procession back to the City was joyous, colourful and noisy, the stately barges 'echoing with the most harmonious wind musick, flutes, hoboys [hautboys, oboes] and trumpets, adorned with streamers, flags and banners'. As the flotilla rowed past Whitehall Palace, it was acknowledged by King James with some apprehension: this was the first Lord Mayor's Day for the Catholic King. On reaching the City, the new Lord Mayor, Sir Robert Geffery, was saluted at Blackfriars Stairs by three volleys from members of the Honourable Artillery Company, 'all adorn'd in their martial ornaments, in buff and shining headpieces, many whereof are of massy silver'.[10] Crowds lined the streets, cheering, and jostling to see their civic leaders in all their finery.

The wooden ostrich carved for Thomas Dekker's mayoral pageant for Sir James Cambell, 1629. A larger version featured in Sir Robert Geffery's mayoral pageant, 1685

The four pageants devised for Geffery's Lord Mayor's Day in 1685 celebrated 'London's Annual Triumph' and were presented at intervals along Cheapside. The Ironmongers' Company, King Edward IV, King James II and Sir Robert Geffery featured large and there were repeated references to the strength and qualities of iron. The significance of the imagery would have been appreciated by Ironmongers, especially the figures of Vulcan, the Roman god of fire and metal-working, and Polyphemus (one of the Cyclops), a giant with one eye who stood at the entrance to a cave with an iron crowbar in one hand (to break the rocks that hindered access to the mines below) and wielding a sword in the other (to prevent all but Ironmongers from entering). The third pageant, the triumphal Arch of Loyalty, extolled Geffery's commitment to the monarchy with the figure of Loyalty swathed in a purple robe, brandishing a shield inscribed *Jacobus Imperator*. A spacious sea chariot alluded to Geffery's overseas trading activities; a sea-lion pointed to his affiliations with the East India Company whose armorial bearings were supported by imaginary sea-lions, and a large 'estridge' (ostrich) derived from the token of the East India Company. On a whimsical note, the ostrich was biting a horse-shoe (ostriches were said to have cast-iron digestions, so could swallow iron, and horse-shoes were staple items of ironmongery). Two models of ostriches had featured in the playwright Anthony Munday's pageant for Sir Sebastian Harvey in 1618 and one appeared in Thomas Dekker's pageant for Sir James Cambell in 1629 (it is still to be seen perching on the staircase at Ironmongers' Hall). The ostriches of 1618 and 1629 were outdone on Lord Mayor's Day 1685 by 'a golden estridge of a vast prodigious size, holding a horse-shoe in its beak, upon the back of which is placed a comely youth of a ruddy, fair complexion'.[11]

As Geffery processed from one pageant to the next, he was greeted by the virtues of the monarchy and the City, lauded in verse and visually represented by eight women 'of majestic mien and beautiful features', dressed as Victory, Triumph, Honour, Peace, Plenty, Courage, Vigilance and Conduct. As Geffery admired Victory, she addressed him 'in twenty-two vile doggerel lines, that had a meaning no doubt; but it was admirably concealed by the Poet'.[12] The poetry may have been tedious but it had to be acknowledged that the performance as a whole was 'more than usually magnificent'.[13] The charges for Geffery's Lord Mayor's Day amounted to £473 (nearly £65,000 at 2012 values);[14] after the cost of the pageants (£175), the most expensive bill was for flags and streamers (£140), with just £10 going to Taubman.[15]

The climax of the day was a splendid dinner at Grocers' Hall, recently enlarged and beautified by Sir John Moore (Lord Mayor 1682–3) 'so as to make it the most commodious seat for the chief magistrate of the city, or a mansion house'[16] (the official Mansion House was not built until the mid-eighteenth century). At the Lord Mayor's dinner, the most ostentatious event in the City's calendar, Sir Robert Geffery was host to King James and Queen Mary, Princess Anne (the future Queen) and her husband, Prince George of Denmark, 'the Lords of His Majesty's Privy Council, with many others of the Nobility, Judges, and other Persons of Quality'.[17] During the feasting, musicians and singers serenaded the diners with a sycophantic ballad addressed to the King, toasting

> 'A Health to that One who Heav'n to the Throne
> Did in spite of Pretenders restore;
> May the friends of the Crown be install'd with Renown
> And his Enemies hang at the Door'.

Then came a unique rendition of the Ironmongers' song — ten verses in praise of iron, 'our subterranean gem', 'the ancient'st of trades', followed by a bawdy composition celebrating the King's accession to the throne.[18]

Considering his unpopularity as Duke of York, the accession of King James II passed smoothly and his entertainment by the Lord Mayor, Sir Robert Geffery, and the City in October 1685 gave the impression that relations between the King and his subjects were amicable. Before the year was out, all had changed. The spectacle of the King and Queen processing to mass, the increasing number of Catholic priests in the capital and the King's imposition of taxes on wines, vinegar, sugar, tobacco and silks alienated Protestants, merchants and the populace alike. King James proved incorrigible and merely responded to mounting opposition by proroguing Parliament, which offended the Lords and the House of Commons. Without Parliament the King pursued his Catholic policies unchecked.

My Lord Mayor's year

As The Rt Hon. The Lord Mayor of London, a title conferred by King Edward III in the fourteenth century, Geffery was the chief magistrate of the City, the head of the oldest surviving municipal corporation in the world and the holder of an office that has existed since the late twelfth century. Within the City boundaries he ranked above everyone except the sovereign, and his status was enhanced by magnificent robes, a chain of office dating from the sixteenth century, and a ceremonial sword that was carried before him by his sword-bearer. He was supported by a team of servants and assistants: the common cryer, common huntsman, two water bailiffs, a serjeant carver, the serjeant and a yeoman of the channel, a yeoman of the chamber, a meal-weigher, a yeoman of the wood-wharf, a fruit-weigher, a hall-keeper, and young men were in attendance; on formal occasions he was accompanied by musicians and a bevy of officials from Guildhall. The pomp and ceremony surrounding the Lord Mayor inspired awe and admiration for one who combined the roles of coroner, conservator of the Thames, Admiral of the port of London, chief magistrate, chief butler at the coronation and head of the Court of Aldermen, which had long been a force to be reckoned with in domestic politics and which was now emerging as a decisive power in the commerce and trade of the City.

The proceedings of the first meeting of the Court of Aldermen under Geffery's leadership, on 10 November 1685, were recorded in heavy black ink under the heading *coram egregio et spectatissimo viro, Roberto Geffery milites maiore civitatis London* (in the presence of the outstanding and most esteemed Robert Geffery, knight, mayor of the City of London). Geffery had nine years' experience of the workings of the Court of Aldermen where, as Lord Mayor, he found himself surrounded by the familiar faces of Aldermen Henry Tulse, Charles Duncombe, James Smyth, William Turner and Peter Rich. In the year ahead, Lord Mayor Geffery faced a punishing schedule of sermons, services, ceremonies and dinners, in addition to the serious business of the Court of Aldermen and the City Corporation. He was confronted immediately by the dictates of King James II in the form of interminable lists of names of the Masters, Wardens and liverymen of the City companies, as approved by the King.[19] Then came a missive instructing him to be watchful on 5 November. The Catholic King would have no truck with fires burning effigies of Guy Fawkes or the Pope, so 'to prevent disorders', bonfires and fireworks were banned, the royal standard was raised on the Tower of London where guns were fired to demonstrate the King's authority, shops were shut and sermons were preached in the churches.[20]

In December it was beholden to the City to provide an escort for Henry Hyde, second Earl of Clarendon (1638–1709), brother of James's first wife, Anne Hyde (1637–71). Clarendon had recently been appointed Lord Lieutenant of Ireland and his send-off demanded a fanfare. Geffery delegated escort duty to 'the Sheriffs in their scarlet gowns on horseback', who were ordered to meet Clarendon at Temple Bar and ride with him through the City to mark his departure for Dublin, via Chester.[21] Clarendon, an Anglican, was entrusted with the task of replacing Protestants with Catholics in key positions in Ireland – a hint of King James's wider intentions. It was a near impossible task and Clarendon earned the King's displeasure and was recalled from Ireland in 1687.

During Geffery's mayoralty, the Court of Aldermen was preoccupied with the building, improvement and regulation of the City's markets at Newgate, Honey Lane, Leadenhall and Woolchurch (the Stocks Market); there were proposals for a new meat market beside the Fleet Ditch and a new lease to the Farmers of the

Markets had to be negotiated. Encroachments on the Thames, property disputes, the weight of the penny wheaten loaf, carts blocking the streets, rulings and precepts for the livery companies, licensing and City appointments were dealt with. There were individual cases to be adjudicated and the care, education and inheritances of orphans to be settled. Even the whims of the Lady Mayoress had to be considered (Geffery was of course a widower, so would have invited a consort to act as Lady Mayoress, most probably his unmarried niece, Katherine, who was his companion and housekeeper in later years). She had her eye on a French chef, Lawrence Renant, who needed to be admitted to the Cooks' Company in order to work for her and Sir Robert. The Court of Aldermen condoned this, also agreeing to the services of William Druce as the Mayoress's haberdasher, and to the delivery of the customary quota of lobsters for the mayoral dining table.[22]

FEARS OF CATHOLIC DOMINATION

Through his chief ministers, King James II summoned Geffery in order to issue him with instructions on matters such as the collection of taxes, the pursuit of conspirators and the suppression of riots in the City. Conspiracies and riots dogged Geffery's mayoral year, the reason being the deep-seated aversion to Roman Catholicism among the City's population. Catholicism conjured up fears of domination by a foreign power, fears that had been stoked by King Charles II's alliance with Louis XIV, who in 1685 revoked the Edict of Nantes, leading to an exodus of Huguenots (French Protestants), many of whom arrived in London with alarming details of their persecution. On the publication of *An Account of the Persecution of the French Protestants* in May 1686, deploring Louis XIV's treatment of the Huguenots, King James commanded Geffery to have copies of the book burned by the executioner in front of Guildhall and at the Royal Exchange.

Londoners associated catholicism with foreigners, with 'Bloody Mary' (Mary Tudor, who had ordered the burning of Protestants), with Guy Fawkes and the gunpowder plot to blow up Parliament in 1605, and many blamed the Great Fire of 1666 on 'the treachery and malice of the Papists'.[23] Conspiracies, such as the plot to kill Charles II, massacre Protestants and place the Duke of York and Jesuits in power, as conjured up by Titus Oates in 1678, had incited the murder of Catholics. When Oates was revealed as a liar and his plot as an invention, he was arrested, tried, then dragged and whipped through the streets of the City and imprisoned (he was released in 1689).

Fears of Catholic plots and possibly the catholicisation of England were not confined to the prejudiced and often unruly rabble. There were valid reasons for believing that England would soon be dominated by Catholics. At Court, in

Titus Oates, perpetrator
of a Jesuit plot to murder
King Charles II, was
found guilty of perjury
and was dragged and
whipped behind a cart
through the streets of
London, May 1685

the army, at the universities and in the capital, Catholics were gaining ground. In January 1686, the King made it plain that he wanted to see Catholic chapels, schools and a printing press established to encourage conversions to the faith. He underestimated the strength of the Protestant opposition to such measures. Despite the quartering of soldiers in the taverns and alehouses of Fleet Street and Salisbury Court, it proved impossible to suppress anti-Catholic rioters, who engendered fear and insecurity, and this had a detrimental effect on trade. During and after the riots associated with the Lime Street 'mass-house' in the spring of 1686 (see pages 136–140), dealings on the Royal Exchange came to a standstill and the Commissioners of the Customs reported that receipts from the port of London fell by thousands of pounds.[24]

TITUS OATES WORT OP DEFERENTE RYSEN VREESELYCK GEGEESELT OM VELE VALSCHE GETUYGEN GEDAEN TEGEN DESE SEVEN BOVEN STAENDE PATERS DER SOCIETEYT IESV. EN ANDERE CATHOLIICKEN TOT LONDEN DEN. 26 MEY 1685.

Although crowds had witnessed the execution of the Duke of Monmouth, rumours were rife that he had escaped and that an impersonator had been executed in his stead. Early in 1686, the King's ministers received intelligence that Monmouth was in the Low Countries, planning another invasion, and, later in the year, a man claiming to be Monmouth was found in hiding, ten miles from central London. As Lord Mayor, Geffery was expected to investigate anything and anyone suspicious in his domain. A warrant issued by King James in March directed that 'all suspected places in and about the City of London and Southwark' must be searched for rebels.[25] Again in May, 'treasonous and seditious libels thrown up and down the streets of London and Westminster' warranted house-to-house searches and the apprehension of guilty persons.[26]

Alarms, plots and rumours prompted a show of force by the King in the summer of 1686. Cannons were dragged from the Tower of London to Hounslow Heath, where fourteen foot battalions were camped with thirty-two squadrons of horse – 13,000 fighting men in all. Londoners were not intimidated. Hounslow Heath was traditionally a popular resort in the summer and the military camp was soon transformed into a fair where apprentices and 'painted women from Whitefriars' enjoyed cavorting, drinking and gambling with the troops.[27]

Shortly before Geffery's mayoral year reached its conclusion, King James ordered the City to celebrate the defeat of the Turks by the army of the Holy League at Buda in September 1686. Geffery, the Aldermen and City officials were commanded to attend a service of thanksgiving at St Mary-le-Bow, in Geffery's Ward. However, the official orders for thanksgiving were transgressed by the anti-papist lobby, 'a great tumult', who lit fires and stoned the Spanish ambassador's house.[28] The Foot Guards were called out and ringleaders were committed to Newgate Prison.[29] This was followed by the usual outbursts of anti-popery on 5 November, 'riotous and disorderly proceedings' in the City, which prompted the King to send for the Lord Mayor and Aldermen, who were rebuked for not having kept the mischief-makers in check. By this time Geffery had been succeeded as Lord Mayor by Sir John Peake; nevertheless, as one of the Aldermen summoned before the King, he was reprimanded.

LORD CHANCELLOR GEORGE JEFFREYS

Lord Chancellor Jeffreys was Robert Geffery's ally in the pursuit of conspirators. The Lord Chancellor was a skilled and voluble lawyer, 'noisy in nature... turbulent...full of tricks', renowned for 'every night drinking until 2 o'clock or beyond that time and that he went to his chamber drunk'.[30] Having sentenced the perpetrators of the Rye House Plot of 1683 and presided over the 'Bloody Assizes' of 1685, Jeffreys faced a challenge with the trial of Henry Booth, Lord Delamere, at Westminster Hall in January 1686. Delamere, charged with high treason for planning a rising against the King, was as cunning as Jeffreys and he achieved an acquittal.

Delamere's acquittal angered the King and was an embarrassment to the Lord Chancellor. Feeling the need of solace perhaps, Jeffreys invited Sir Robert Geffery and Sir John Reresby (1634–89, another staunch royalist) to dinner a few days after the trial. It was a raucous evening, during which Lord Chancellor Jeffreys, 'haveing drunke smartly at dinner (which was his custome)', called for the comedian, Mountfort, to entertain the party. William Mountfort was a clever

OPPOSITE
Lord Chancellor George Jeffreys, Baron Jeffreys of Wem. Painted by John Michael Wright when Jeffreys was the City's Common Serjeant, 1675

Sir George Jeffreys
Recorder of the City
of London, Sixth
Son of John Jeffreys
Esq. of Acton in
the County of
Denbigh.

mimic and he gave impressions of the principal lawyers of the day, causing much hilarity.[31] Jeffreys and Geffery had been friends and colleagues for many years, and one of the latter's first initiatives as Lord Mayor had been to commission a portrait of Jeffreys by Sir Godfrey Kneller, to be hung at Guildhall. This no longer hangs at Guildhall, however two portraits of Jeffreys by Kneller (c.1685–6) survive, one at Harvard University Law School and another at Erddig, a National Trust property in Wales near Jeffreys's birthplace.

In addition to Robert Geffery and John Reresby, the Lord Chancellor's cronies included the merchant, John Jeffreys (c.1659–1715), the Whig banker, Sir Robert Clayton (1629–1707), the Whig lawyer, Henry Pollexfen (1632–91) and Alderman Charles Duncombe, (1648–1711), a wealthy banker whose business was based at the sign of The Grasshopper in Lombard Street. Although fiercely partisan himself, the Lord Chancellor enjoyed the company of a wide circle of friends with differing political views. Duncombe hosted a dinner in 1688, when the party indulged in 'a great debauch of wine', drinking 'to that height' that they stripped to their shirts and tried to climb a sign post to toast the King's health.[32] It is not recorded whether Robert Geffery was present on that occasion but it is likely; Lord Chancellor Jeffreys certainly was.

Geffery and Jeffreys were united in their loyalty to the Stuarts until, in 1687, their paths diverged. Over the previous two years, Robert Geffery's loyalty to King James II had been severely tested by the King's policies (Thomas à Becket in 1170 and Thomas More in 1534 had faced a parallel dilemma). Ultimately, Geffery's commitment to the Anglican Church triumphed over all else, resulting in his dismissal from aldermanic office in 1687. Whereas Lord Chancellor Jeffreys's loyalty to the King over-rode any religious scruples he may have had, and the second Earl of Sunderland (1641–1702, Secretary of State and Lord President) converted to catholicism to placate James, Robert Geffery stood firm in his faith.

THE KING'S AGENT

King James II relied on Lord Chancellor Jeffreys, known to be merciless, and the Earl of Sunderland, nicknamed 'the popish dog' on his conversion to catholicism, to enforce his policies nationally. As Lord Mayor, Robert Geffery was the King's chief tool in the City of London, although at odds with the King's catholicism; for example, in January 1686 the King dismissed Henry Compton, the feisty Bishop of London, from the Privy Council – a personal insult and a stab at the Church of England that would have vexed Geffery. With the inhabitants of the City in rebellious mood, the King threatened to send infantry regiments to quell anti-Catholic riots if necessary. Knowing full well that this would inflame the situation, Geffery and his brother Aldermen procrastinated. 'It is said they have not shown much inclination' (to agree to the presence of troops), the Dutch ambassador reported laconically.[33]

The careers of both Lord Chancellor Jeffreys and Sir Robert Geffery were promoted by the Earl of Sunderland. Shortly before Geffery was installed as Lord Mayor in 1685, Sunderland alerted the City authorities to 'some ill practices amongst the dissaffected party' (opponents of the King) about which His Majesty 'would have you more watchful'.[34] The alarm had been sounded by a letter claiming that 22,000 Londoners supported the Duke of Monmouth's rebellion. Sunderland and his fellow Secretary of State, the Earl of Middleton (1649/50–1719), relied on Geffery to act as a spy in the City and to inform them of anything or anybody suspicious. When rumours circulated of another rebellion (following the Duke of Monmouth's failed attempt) and evidence emerged of a scheme to assassinate the King on his way to Edinburgh, Middleton contacted Geffery. As yet Geffery had 'nothing worthy of communicating' to the Secretary of State, but he returned his 'humble and hearty thanks' to His Majesty for the offer of 'business'.[35] Middleton had been alerted to 'a serious rebellion before or about midsummer and that the Duke of Monmouth's living and goes about in woman's cloathes in Bristol and Somerset'.[36] Letters were soon intercepted by a wider network and forwarded to Geffery via his friend and executor, Sir William Russell of Lombard Street, letters containing 'dangerous and dreadful words' and relating to 'a scandalous libel'. Other correspondence 'of dangerous consequence' from 'a cockbrained woman' had fallen into the hands of Mr Alderson, a minister who contacted Geffery.[37] Some of the intelligence passed to Geffery related to William Strode and George Speke, both of whom were well-known conspirators and leaders of the opposition to the King in Somerset.

Secrecy also pervaded meetings of the Court of Aldermen which debated 'some great affaires of this citie' in March 1686, affairs that were too sensitive to be minuted in the proceedings. The Aldermen had complete confidence in Geffery to deal with the matter: 'This Court taking the same into serious consideration doth absolutely refer all to the Rt Hon. the Lord Mayor', who was 'fully empowered with the advice of such Aldermen as his Lordship shall think fit to consult, to give such orders and take and pursue such course and means for the Honour and service of this City as His Lordship shall think fitting'. The trust placed in Geffery was stressed by a note in the margin, 'Lord Mayor absolutely impowered in a great affair'.[38] The secrecy and seriousness surrounding this 'great affair' pointed to fears of an uprising in the City and plans to assassinate King James, posing a serious threat to the security of London and the kingdom.

RIOTS AT THE LIME STREET 'MASS-HOUSE'

Forty years after the destruction of the Cheapside cross, the prohibition of sports on Sundays, the closure of theatres and all that a Puritan regime entailed, Roman Catholic priests paraded the streets of London dressed in their distinctive garb, and Catholic chapels opened. During King Charles II's reign, members of the royal family had worshipped discreetly at their Catholic chapels at St James's Palace and Somerset House, and private chapels could be found at the residences of foreign ambassadors and merchants. With the accession of James II, catholicism was no longer discreet: within the first two days of his reign, the

One from a pack of playing cards, illustrating Trained Bands guarding 'ye Mass hous' near Geffery's house in Lime Street. The Catholic chapel or 'mass-house' was targeted by the mob in 1686. As the current Lord Mayor, Geffery, accompanied by Aldermen and the militia, tried to disperse the rioters

King went publicly to mass with his Italian Queen. Sir Christopher Wren was commissioned to design a Catholic chapel at Whitehall Palace (1685–7) and the King encouraged the Catholic clergy to found new chapels, colleges and schools in London and throughout the kingdom. A convent opened at Clerkenwell on the site of the ancient cloister of St John, the Franciscans opened a chapel near the Dominicans at Lincoln's Inn Fields, Benedictine monks colonised St James's Palace while the Jesuits (who had been banned from the capital in 1648) were represented at Court, at the Savoy, Bucklersbury and Lime Street.

All this was an abomination to Protestant Londoners and to conservative Anglicans such as Geffery. When in the spring of 1686, a 'mass-house' was set up in Lime Street, Geffery anticipated that it would provoke riots, so shut it, which angered King James. The King had personally encouraged James Stamford/ Stanford, the envoy of the Elector Palatine, to establish a chapel in the City, pointing to a large mansion in Lime Street (opposite Geffery's house but further north) as a suitable site. The King subscribed £600 towards the setting up of the chapel and assured Stamford of military protection should there be trouble. Stamford threw himself into the project with gusto, reporting to the Elector that a large ambassadorial residence and chapel in the heart of the City of London befitted his status as a Catholic prince.[39]

Henry Compton, Bishop of London, Edward Stillingfleet, Dean of St Paul's and Sir Robert Geffery (it was rumoured that opposition to the chapel was stirred by this triumvirate) looked on with trepidation as workmen built a potential hub of Roman Catholicism just a short distance from the Anglican churches of St Dionis, Backchurch and St Andrew, Undershaft. As the chapel neared completion, threatening crowds gathered and in order to avoid a riot, Geffery and the Sheriffs ordered the workmen away, shut the building and confiscated the keys, at the same time 'affronting and giving ill language to the say'd Resident's servants'.[40] Stamford complained to the King, who ordered both Stamford and Geffery to appear before him and the Privy Council – on a Sunday. After Stamford had made his case, Geffery presented a strong defence. He explained that he had closed the building in order to avoid a riot. He claimed that the chapel was illegal and without precedent. He informed King James that it was 'without example that ever a foreign minister residing in the City had exercised the popish religion but only in Westminster, and consequently he [Stamford] was the more blameable, being an Englishman by birth' (as opposed to a foreign merchant or diplomat, who was entitled to practise his religion while in England).[41] King James thanked Geffery for taking precautions 'to prevent all apprehended mischief', but insisted that Stamford was at liberty 'to do in his own house as he thinks right', and that it was Geffery's duty to protect Stamford from the mob.

This evaded the issue, the point being that the Lime Street chapel had been built not just for the private use of Stamford and the Elector, but 'for the service of the Roman Church', with Catholic merchants, their households and converts in mind.[42] Furthermore it had been judged illegal by 'the ablest gentlemen of the long robe' (judges and lawyers).[43] Dismissing legal opinion, James insisted that the chapel be re-opened. He instructed Geffery to return the keys and, in the presence of Lord Chancellor Jeffreys and the Privy Council, the King rebuked Geffery: 'Take heed what you do. Obey me; and do not trouble yourself either about gentlemen of the long robe or gentlemen of the short robe' (the reference to gentlemen of the short robe seems to refer to anyone other than the judges and lawyers 'of the long robe'). To add to his humiliation, Geffery was then reprimanded by his friend the Lord Chancellor, who berated him 'with the genuine eloquence of the Old Bailey Bar'.[44]

So the Lime Street chapel opened on Sunday 18 April 1686 and, as Geffery had anticipated, there was a commotion. Crowds assembled, the priests were mocked and apprentices broke into the chapel; one foolhardy apprentice boasted that he would 'break their crosses and juggling-boxes [confessionals?] down'.[45] Geffery, who had 'taken all imaginable cares to quell and suppress the rabble' appeared in person, accompanied by Aldermen and the militia, to subdue the uproar.[46] There were some twenty arrests, but one aggressive apprentice escaped and a priest was injured. Geffery was later castigated by the Privy Council and warned that if, as Lord Mayor, he could not keep the peace, the King would send his Foot Guards to do so.[47] Anxious to avoid further violence, Geffery ordered the City militia to be watchful, advised citizens to ensure their apprentices behaved themselves and he assured Stamford that 'he had taken upon himself to prevent all apprehended danger'.[48] Despite Geffery's efforts, the London 'hotheads' (apprentices) plundered a crucifix from the chapel and set it up beside the parish pump, 'paying a very disorderly adoration of it with hollowing', and 'saying they would have no wooden gods worshipped there, frighting the priest but not hurting him'. Once more, Lord Mayor Geffery rushed to the scene, to be greeted with cries of 'No wooden gods! What! Is the Lord Mayor of our City come to preach us Popery? No, sure it cannot be'. The militia was called out to disperse the demonstrators, but on hearing that the purpose of the riot was to attack a Catholic chapel, the soldiers expressed sympathy with the rioters and withdrew, muttering 'We cannot in conscience fight for Popery'.[49]

With the King's backing, the Lime Street 'mass-house' stood as a beacon of Roman Catholicism in the City and a source of curiosity that attracted sightseers. Stamford reported to the Elector that it was the largest and finest of London's Catholic chapels: 'the chapel is already famous', he wrote, 'all Christendom speaks

LEFT
Father Charles Petre
preached at the Lime
Street 'mass-house' in
1688, provoking a riot.
One from a pack of
playing cards

RIGHT
Father Edward Petre Bt,
King James II's Jesuit
confessor, *c.*1688

of it'.[50] Famous or infamous? Sunday worshippers were abused by onlookers, who pelted them with mud and sprinkled them with 'stinking sewage stuff', signifying holy water. Defying all opposition, King James ordered the Jesuits to take over the chapel, under the leadership of Father Charles Petre (1645–1712), the younger brother of the King's personal confessor, Father Edward Petre (1631–99). With customary zeal, the Jesuits established schools in Westminster, at the Savoy and adjoining the Lime Street chapel, for the instruction of children. Supported by the King with an annual stipend for its upkeep by seven Jesuit priests, the Lime Street school developed into a thriving college and missionary post: during the course of two years the Jesuits of Lime Street claimed to have 'reconciled' 200 souls to the Roman Catholic religion.[51]

LE ROY IACQUE DÉLOGE.

J'avois fait un ragoust pour tout L'Angleterre:
sans que ie me suis trop hasté'.
J'aurois demon renom rempli toutte la terre;
Mais un ORANGE a tout gâté'.

As opposition to the King and Catholics escalated, the Lime Street chapel was the target of another attack by the mob on 9 October 1688, while the priests celebrated mass. Father Charles Petre, 'an impertinent Jesuit who in their Masse-house the Sunday before had disparaged the scripture and railed at our Translation [the English translation of the Bible] with extraordinary ignorance and impudence which some present contradicting, they pulled him out of the Pulpit and treated him very coarsely in so much as it was likely to create a very great disturbance in the city'.[52] Father Petre was fortunate to escape to the house of a neighbouring merchant where he hid until the tumult abated. Ultimately, Geffery won the day: the Lime Street 'mass-house' was officially closed, then demolished by the violent mob in the wake of King James's flight to France in December 1688.

'TURNED OUT'

By the Declaration of Indulgence of 1687 (issued in Scotland in February, in England in April), King James II suspended penal laws against Catholics, dissenters and nonconformists. By so doing he hoped to secure wide support in establishing Catholic emancipation, which of course alarmed Anglicans. In an attempt to ensure that the City supported the King's policies, Lord Chancellor Jeffreys made an appointment with the Court of Aldermen in June 1687. His brief was to impress the leaders of the City that Aldermen and Sheriffs must be royalists and to stress that all candidates for vacancies must have the King's approval. At least six Aldermen had asked to be discharged from office, claiming they could not afford the expense of the mayoralty which they would incur in due course. In truth, they wished to resign because they could no longer stomach the King's Catholic policies, 'times are becoming rather delicate for them', the Dutch ambassador hinted.[53] These Aldermen did not have long to wait before being relieved of their duties. In August 1687 King James dismissed several of them in a purge that extended to all officers and liverymen of the City of London whose attachment to the Church of England and whose horror of popery was evident. Thus Sir Peter Rich, Sir William Russell, Sir William Pritchard, Sir John Moore, Sir Henry Tulse, Sir Robert Geffery and likeminded Aldermen were dismissed, and over 1,000 liverymen of the City companies were expunged from the lists. As the Earl of Ailesbury lamented, 'All the jolly genteel citizens are turned out, and all sneaking fanatics put in...At the Guildhall those worthy Aldermen excluded were looked on as scally sheep [a scall was a leprous scab]...These truly worthy, and loyal and discarded magistrates I presented to the King and named each. The King gave them his hand to kiss, and with a most smiling face said gracious things to every one, and called Sir James Smith [Smyth] his old fellow fox-hunter. I let fall a word that I hoped to see them restored by His Majesty'. The King had dismissed these 'truly worthy' Aldermen from office, yet he entertained them to dinner and cajoled them, in the vain hope that they would remain loyal. 'This feast was magnificent but to me it was a very melancholy one', concluded the Earl of Ailesbury, who came close to resigning his commission over the issue.[54]

Among the 'sneaking fanatics' who replaced the 'jolly genteel citizens' were William Kiffin, a Baptist minister now elevated to Alderman in place of Sir Samuel Dashwood, and Sir John Shorter, an Anabaptist, who was now Lord Mayor. The King's policy extended to the City livery companies, the motive being to place 'other persons' in the companies, 'thereby if possible the more easily to procure a favourable election of members for the ensuing parliament' (members who would support the King), as the Dutch ambassador explained to the Prince of Orange.[55] An order of the King and Privy Council was received at Ironmongers' Hall in September 1687, informing the Company that 'His Majesty has thought fitt' to remove and displace the Master, John Grice, the two Wardens, also Sir Robert Geffery and all the Court of Assistants.[56] Thus Geffery received a second demotion and Captain William Walker (who had been supplanted, protesting, by the King's appointment of Geffery in 1685) was installed as Master. Geffery did not protest at his dismissal from the Ironmongers' Court. He chose to keep a low profile and did not reappear at Ironmongers' Hall until after the Prince of Orange had landed at Torbay in November 1688.

'DOWN-RIGHT POPERY'[57]

Meanwhile there was no restraining King James. Catholics were appointed to the 'Popish Cabinet Council', as the Dutch ambassador described it,[58] and anyone who could not be relied upon to back the King's policies was dismissed from office. The King and Lord Chancellor Jeffreys revived the Ecclesiastical Commission as a tool to suppress dissent and tighten control over recalcitrant Anglicans, beginning with the suspension of Henry Compton, Bishop of London. The Commission then turned its attention to that stronghold of Anglicanism, the University of Oxford. The Fellows of Magdalen College having refused to accept the King's nominee as President, the Ecclesiastical Commission forcibly installed Samuel Parker, who had been appointed Bishop of Oxford by King James in 1686. As President of Magdalen from 1687 Parker was under orders to favour Catholics as Fellows of the College. The tense situation enraged him, prompting a stroke from which he died at the age of forty-eight after just one year at Magdalen.

Determined to enforce his will and discipline the Anglican Church, in May 1688 the King ordered the clergy to proclaim the Declaration of Indulgence in their churches. When the Archbishop of Canterbury and six bishops petitioned against this, the King committed them to the Tower of London to await prosecution for seditious libel. Their rapid acquittal was a victory for the established Church: bells were rung, effigies of the Pope were burned and glasses were raised to 'the confusion and distraction of the Papists', much to the King's chagrin.[59]

With the birth of a son and heir in June 1688, King James's position seemed impregnable. After many miscarriages and infant deaths, the Queen gave birth to James Francis Edward Stuart, Prince of Wales; 'The Catholics show themselves exceedingly pleased', the Dutch ambassador observed.[60] However, the prospect of a continuing Catholic monarchy inspired a revolution: within three weeks of the birth of the King's heir, a note was delivered to the Protestant Prince William of Orange, inviting him to accept the throne of England. When, in September, James learned that Prince William had responded positively and was making military and naval preparations for an invasion of England, he back-tracked. In a desperate attempt to curry favour, he wooed the City of London, its Lord Mayor, Aldermen and inhabitants by restoring the City's charter and reinstating the Aldermen, including Geffery, whom he had expelled the previous year. In a further move to bolster his position and ensure the future of the Stuart monarchy, the King summoned the Privy Council, the Archbishop of Canterbury, Judges, the Lord Mayor and Aldermen to swear to the legality of his son's birth (it was rumoured that the baby had been smuggled into the Queen's bedchamber in a warming pan). The Queen, her midwife and attendants were present to vouch for the genuine birth of the baby, giving evidence to the assembly of chief ministers, Aldermen of the City and the King's Jesuit confessor, Father Edward Petre (the Earl of Clarendon at first declined the summons on account of the Jesuit's presence). Among the Aldermen stood Geffery, who confirmed the legitimacy of James Francis Edward Stuart as the rightful successor to the throne of England, Ireland and Scotland. But the Dutch fleet was ready to set sail, waiting only for a favourable wind; the invasion led by Prince William of Orange was imminent.

Endnotes

1 Narcissus Luttrell, *A Brief Historical Relation of State Affairs from September 1678 to April 1714* (1857), rev. edn. 1969, vol I, p.341 2 Nicholl, pp.293–300, provides an English translation of the Charter 3 CMIC, 15, 28 April 1685, GL MS. 16967/7 4 Ibid., 27 April 1699 5 Ibid., 2 July, 18 August 1685 6 Ibid., 2 October, 2, 13 November 1685 7 Dispatches of the Dutch ambassador, 27 July 1685, Add. MS. 34,508, f.65v, BL 8 Ibid., 9 November 1685, f.88 9 An original copy of Matthew Taubman's pageant, *London's Annual Triumph* (1685), survives at the British Library. The pageant and the events of the day are described by Nicholl, pp.305–21 10 Nicholl, p.310 11 Ibid., pp.183, 311 12 James P. Malcolm, *Londinium Redivivum* (1803), vol II, pp.45–7. The Ironmongers' Company demanded that the sea lion, two sea horses and the ostrich be returned to the Hall after the 1629 pageant. Mr Christmas negotiated to keep the sea horses, the sea lion cannot be found. See Robert Withington, *English Pageantry* (1920), vol II, pp.38, 40 13 Ibid., p.47 14 Figures derived from E.H. Phelps Brown and Sheila V. Hopkins, 'Seven centuries of the prices of consumables compared with builders' wage rates', *Economica*, November 1956, and the UK Retail Price Index 2012, www. wolfbane.com/rpi 15 An Account of the Charges on Lord Mayor's Day 29 October 1685, GL MS. 17081, f.342 16 W. Herbert, *The History of the Twelve Great Livery Companies of London* (1837), vol I, p.347 17 *London Gazette*, 2 November 1685 18 Nicholl, pp.305–21 19 28 October 1685, Rep 90 20 SPD, 5 November 1685 p.377 21 15 December 1685, Rep 91 22 Ibid., 28 November 1685, 1 June 1686 23 In 1680 the Court of Common Council ordered an inscription to this effect for the Monument to the Great Fire 24 T.B. Macaulay, *The History of England* (1858), vol II, p.101 25 SPD, 24 March 1686, p.85 26 Ibid., 22 May 1686, p.137 27 Macaulay, op.cit., p.102 28 Narcissus Luttrell, op.cit., p.385 29 SPD, 10 September 1686, p.261 30 Roger North, *The Lives of the Norths*, ed. A. Jessopp (1890), vol I, p.277 31 *Memoirs of Sir John Reresby*, ed. Andrew Browning (1991), p.408 32 G.W. Keeton, *Lord Chancellor Jeffreys and the Stuart Cause* (1965), p.355 33 Dispatches, op. cit., 15 January 1686, Add. MS. 34,508, f.104v, BL 34 SPD, 5 June 1685, p.181 35 Add. MS. 41,804, f. 180, BL 36 Ibid., ff.168–9 37 Ibid., ff.177, 179, 214 38 18 March 1686, Rep 90 39 Gregory Macdonald, 'The Lime Street Chapel 1686–88', *Dublin Review* (1927), vol 180, pp.253–65 and vol 181, pp.1–16 40 Privy Council Registers, vol LXXI, 26 March 1686, TNA 41 Dispatches, op. cit., 9 April 1686, Add. MS. 34,508, ff.110v–111, BL 42 Narcissus Luttrell, op.cit., p.373 43 T.B. Macaulay, op. cit., p.100 44 Ibid., p.101 45 *The Ellis Correspondence*, ed. G.A. Ellis (1829), vol I, 20 April 1686, p.111 46 Add. MS. 72, 595, ff.66–66v, BL 47 *The Ellis Correspondence*, op. cit., 27 March, 27 April 1686, pp.83–4, 118–9 48 Dispatches, op. cit., ff.112v–113 49 *The Ellis Correspondence*, op. cit., 27 April 1686, pp.118–9 50 *Dublin Review*, op cit. (1927), vol 181, pp.1–16 51 Henry Foley, *Records of the English Province of the Society of Jesus* (1879), vol V, pp.263–77. See also T.G. Holt, 'A Jesuit School in the City in 1688', *Transactions London and Middlesex Archaeological Society* (1981), vol 32, pp.153–5 52 JE, vol IV, 7 October 1688, p.599 53 Dispatches, op. cit., 17 May 1685, Add. MS. 34,508, f.115, BL 54 *Memoirs of Thomas, Earl of Ailesbury* (1890), vol I, pp.175–6 55 Dispatches, op. cit, 26 August 1687, Add. MS. 34,510, f. 49v, BL 56 CMIC, 25 September, 1687, GL MS. 16967/7 57 Andrew Marvell, *An Account of the Growth of Popery and Arbitrary Government in England* (1677), p.69 58 Dispatches, op. cit., 13 July 1688, Add. MS. 34,510, f.138v, BL 59 Ibid., 24 October 1687, f.53 60 Ibid., 22 June 1688, f.127

6 | REVOLUTION

The invasion of England by Prince William of Orange in November 1688, which prompted the flight of James II, his Queen and son to France in December, has gone down in history as a glorious, bloodless revolution, a *coup d'état* – or was it an abdication? To the coalition of Whigs and Tories who invited William to assume the crown it was indeed a glorious revolution. English Protestants likewise celebrated the departure of the Catholic King James and the accession of King William and Queen Mary as glorious. However glorious, the revolution was not bloodless. A skirmish in Somerset resulted in some fifteen to twenty deaths, there were Catholic killings throughout the country, intermittent uprisings by the Jacobites (supporters of James II) in Scotland and much blood was to be shed in Ireland before King William III's victory at the Battle of the Boyne in 1690. In terms of a struggle between the State and the absolutist Stuarts, the events of the winter of 1688–9 were indeed a *coup* and, by fleeing the country, King James could be said to have abdicated. For his part, Prince William of Orange had a claim to the throne of England, Scotland and Ireland both by descent and through his marriage to James's elder daughter, Mary; furthermore, his accession held the promise of a highly desirable Anglo-Dutch alliance against Louis XIV of France.

As a senior Alderman, Sir Robert Geffery was directly involved in the chain of events leading to the revolution of 1688–9. He dealt with anti-Catholic riots; he suffered James's autocratic temper ('Take heed what you do. Obey me') and abrupt dismissal from office in 1687. With the King's last-minute bid to retain the throne, Geffery found himself reinstated with the other 'truly worthy and loyal Aldermen',[1] and he was summoned to testify to the legality of the King's heir, so confirming the Stuart succession. However, the King's decision to leave the country, with the Queen and their son, removed this threat. The Lord Chancellor, George Jeffreys, also decided to flee, but he was arrested, and then imprisoned following an emotional meeting with Geffery. Meanwhile, as the nation teetered between monarchs, the steadying influence of the Archbishop of Canterbury and the 'Humble Address' from the City of London to Prince William of Orange, signed by Geffery and his colleagues, averted anarchy. By Christmas 1688, Prince William was officially in control of the kingdom, shaken though it was by recent events.

The Act of Settlement of 1701 satisfied Geffery, the City of London and all Anglicans that henceforward Catholics were excluded from the throne of England. King James II died in exile that year and King William III died in March 1702. The accession of the Anglican Queen Anne was greeted with national rejoicing: the bells of St Dionis, Geffery's parish church, rang out at her coronation on St George's Day in April, and again in August, when news reached London of Marlborough's victories in the Netherlands, which had forced the French to retreat. This triumphant year saw Sir Robert Geffery in the revered position of Father of the City (see chapter 7).

THE IMPENDING INVASION

PREVIOUS PAGE
'Lime Street Chaple pulling down and burnt' by anti-Catholic protestors, December 1688

OPPOSITE LEFT
Two from a pack of playing cards. The Queen, with her infant son, the Prince of Wales, and Father Petre left London under cover of darkness, December 1688

King James II leaving Whitehall, 18 December 1688

The invitation to Prince William of Orange from the 'immortal seven' (the Earl of Danby, the Earl of Shrewsbury, the Earl of Devonshire, the Bishop of London, Viscount Lumley, Edward Russell and Henry Sydney) was carried with utmost secrecy to Holland in June 1688 by Admiral William Herbert in disguise. This set in motion military preparations for the Dutch invasion of England five months later. When rumours reached London that Prince William had accepted the invitation and was amassing his forces, there was a degree of panic. The Lord Mayor and Aldermen sought an audience with King James, who placated them by vowing to summon Parliament, restore the City of London's franchises and privileges and re-instate the Aldermen he had turned out of office in 1687. This was a last resort by a monarch who now realised he was threatened with deposition by a foreign Prince, who was his nephew and son-in-law (Prince William's mother was the sister of both Charles II and James II, and his wife was Mary, his cousin and the eldest daughter of James II).

Somewhat desperate, James sent his Lord Chancellor to seek a reconciliation with the power-base in the City and so it was that eighteen Aldermen – Sir Robert Geffery, Sir Henry Tulse and all 'the old set' – were re-appointed in October 1688, 'and joy shined in all their faces that they were met together, by His Majesty's grace and favour'.[2] Some of the 'old set' such as Sir Robert Clayton, were weary of His Majesty's volatility, suspecting that as soon as the crisis had passed the King would recant, so they declined re-appointment. Those who did accept the King's olive branch were not exactly effusive in their agreement to resume office, merely conceding to discharge the trust placed in them.

Having reinstated the Aldermen, King James and the Lord Chancellor endeavoured to secure the support of the livery companies. Lord Chancellor Jeffreys invited the Master, Wardens and Assistants of the Ironmongers' Company to his house in Duke Street, Westminster, to regale them with the good news. His Majesty deigned to return to them the charter they had been forced to surrender in 1684 and would grant Letters Patent restoring the Ironmongers' privileges and autonomy. Thus Geffery resumed his former status on the Ironmongers' Court, as on the Court of Aldermen. Pleased to be among old friends once more, he appeared at Ironmongers' Hall on 21 November 1688 after a long absence. Similarly, City officials found themselves back in their posts, the Common Council met after a lapse of five years, the *Quo Warranto* proceedings questioning the status and legality of the City of London were dropped and the City's charter was restored. Lord Chancellor Jeffreys personally carried that prized document through the streets to Guildhall, as crowds cheered. Alderman Sir

Robert Geffery would have been among those assembled to receive it.

Meanwhile, the prospect of the invasion of England by Prince William of Orange raised the danger of local and possibly national insurrections in the event of a confrontation between King James and Prince William. In London, the apprentices began to organise themselves by electing colonels and summoning volunteers to march under banners proclaiming 'No Pope. No Papists'. Coffee-houses closed, newspapers were suppressed and at Ironmongers' Hall armaments were prepared 'in this time of difficulty and hazards'.[3] Trained Bands patrolled the streets of the City and a company of the Orange Regiment guarded the Royal Exchange. Such precautions were justified — the mob moved into action, light-ing a fire at Leadenhall Market, which ignited and destroyed two houses close to Geffery's own, and 'our London boys' (apprentices) 'after the mirth of the Lord Mayor's show', attacked the Catholic chapel at Bucklersbury.[4] This was the first wave of the anti-popery riots on the eve of the revolution.

KING JAMES AND THE LORD CHANCELLOR FLEE

As Londoners waited nervously for the predicted invasion, the river procession on Lord Mayor's Day in October 1688 was subdued. The watermen stayed at home, fearing impressment into the King's army, and citizens barred their doors, fearing riots. Sure enough, anti-Catholic violence erupted and Catholic chapels were set alight. Nevertheless, the new Lord Mayor, Sir John Chapman (who, like Geffery, had been dismissed as an Alderman by the King in 1687 and recently restored), was installed safely, and he promptly entertained Geffery and senior Ironmongers to dinner.

Prince William of Orange landed at Torbay in Devon on 5 November 1688, an auspicious day in the Protestant calendar. On 17 November, King James set out to repel the invader and his army, intending 'to give them no quarter'.[5] However, he did not have the support of the country; neither the aristocracy, the gentry, nor labourers were persuaded to fight for the King. On the contrary, many looked favourably on the invading force, believing that Prince William and his wife, Mary, would save them from popish tyranny.

Having attempted to consolidate his position in London by re-appointing the Aldermen, cancelling the *Quo Warranto* proceedings and restoring the City's charter, King James led his troops (who far outnumbered the invading force) to Salisbury. It soon became apparent that there was little appetite for war and the best regiments were unwilling to fight. That incomparable soldier, Lord Churchill (later the Duke of Marlborough), deserted the King, whose own daughter, Princess Anne, declared for William and Mary, her brother-in-law and sister. Morally defeated and physically debilitated by uncontrollable nosebleeds, James retreated to London to open negotiations with Prince William.

In early December the King's supporters began to leave the country. His chief minister, the despised Earl of Sunderland, left for Rotterdam. On the night of 9/10 December the Queen escaped, disguised as a washerwoman and taking the Prince of Wales with her. King James fled from the capital the following night, throwing the Great Seal of England into the Thames on his way. He was accompanied by Sir Edward Hales, the Roman Catholic Lieutenant of the Tower of London and another Catholic, Ralph Sheldon, who all intended to take refuge on the Continent. Their plans were foiled at Faversham, where they were ambushed by some fishermen on the look-out for priests and plunder. Escorted back to the capital on 16 December, the King was surprised to be greeted by welcoming crowds.

On the day of James's abortive flight, it was the implacable Archbishop of Canterbury, William Sancroft (1617–93), who took the reins, his main concern being to avoid violence. Robert Geffery knew and supported Sancroft, who had been Dean of St Paul's from 1664–78, and had corresponded with him about the desirability of a spire for Christ Church, Newgate Street.[6] Sancroft exerted a calming influence over the peers of the realm, the Lord Mayor and the City during the crisis, with the result that the transition from one monarch to another was conducted in a dignified fashion. On 11 December, the Corporation of London issued a 'Humble Address' to Prince William inviting him to enter the City, and as one of the Aldermen, Geffery heartily endorsed this plea. The document expressed profound relief 'for your appearing in Arms in this Kingdom' and the Prince was implored 'to carry on and perfect your Glorious Design to rescue England, Scotland and Ireland from Slavery and Popery', following 'His Majesty's withdrawing himself'. Prince William was urged 'to Repair to this City where your Highness will be Received with Universal Joy and Satisfaction'.[7] The message was reinforced two days later by Sir Robert Clayton, MP for the City, who delivered loyal addresses from the Common Council and the Lieutenancy of London to Prince William, biding his time in Berkshire.

London's declaration in favour of Prince William was confounded by King James's re-appearance in the capital. But William now had the upper hand and the King agreed to leave the country. He finally departed from London under escort on 18 December, and from Rochester he travelled to join his wife and son at St Germain-en-Laye in France. As John Verney reported, 'The best news' is that 'the King has gone off for the last time escorted by the Prince's Guards'.[8]

As soon as he heard of the King's plans to leave the country, Lord Chancellor Jeffreys also decided that exit was the best strategy. Disguised as a seaman, he

made his way to Wapping to await a boat, but he was recognised by one of his former victims in the courts, who alerted the authorities. Jeffreys was returned to London under guard before the crowds could lynch him. He was then brought before the Lord Mayor, Sir John Chapman. Chapman collapsed, overcome by the sight of the Lord Chancellor of England, dishevelled and in disguise. He 'fell cryeing then into a fit, for which he was blooded and put to Bed. Soe the Lord Mayor being ill he coud not sign any warrant, the L. Chanc. satt downe and ate heartily, but turning about he saw Sr Robt Jefferyes, Late Mayor, who cryed and came to kiss his hand and then the L. Chanc. alsoe cryed, he said what have I done that people are soe violent agst me?'.[9]

This tearful meeting of friends – the former Lord Chancellor Jeffreys and the former Lord Mayor Geffery – was their last. Geffery was visibly moved by the plight of the disgraced Lord Chancellor and was one of the few not to condemn him as he faced incarceration in the Tower of London on charges of treason. Jeffreys had been ill intermittently for many years and he died in the Tower in 1689. His will was replete with repentance of past sins, he denied responsibility for the Ecclesiastical Commission and swore allegiance to the Church of England, 'the best Church in the world'. He appointed his 'well-beloved friends', the merchants Sir Jeffrey Jeffreys and his brother, John Jeffreys, to be his executors and chose, wisely, to be buried quietly and under cover of darkness.[10] For security reasons, his body was not released until 1693, when it was finally laid to rest at St Mary, Aldermanbury.

DESECRATION AND DESTRUCTION

When news broke that the King had left the capital in the early hours of 11 December, the London mob stormed Catholic chapels, houses and even taverns that displayed signs such as 'The Cardinal's Hat' or 'The Nun's Head'. J.P. Malcolm chronicled an account of the violent events of that night: 'No sooner was the King's withdrawing known but the mobile [mob] consulted to wreak their vengeance on papists and popery; and last night began with pulling down and burning the new-built Mass-house near the arch in Lincoln's Inn Fields; thence they went to Wild-House, the residence of the Spanish Ambassador where they ransacked, destroyed and burnt all the ornamental and inside part of the chappel'.[11] St John's, Clerkenwell, was the next target, for it was believed that gridirons, knives and cauldrons for the torture of Protestants were hidden there. The Catholic publishing house at Blackfriars owned by Henry Hills was burnt down and the area of destruction extended to the Haymarket and the papal nuncio's residence. The 'mass-house' in Lime Street, near Sir Robert Geffery's

OPPOSITE
Lord Chancellor George Jeffreys attempted to leave the country, in disguise, December 1688. He was discovered at Wapping, escorted back to London and imprisoned in the Tower of London

house, presented a challenge for it was recently built and sturdy, but the mob vowed 'they would down with it were it as strong as Portsmouth [fortified in preparation for the invasion]. And accordingly having levelled it, they carried all the trumpery in mock procession and triumph with oranges on the tops of swords and staves, with great lighted candles in gilt candlesticks'.[12]

Lime Street Chaple pulling down and burnt

The following night, which went down in memory as 'The Irish Night', was even more alarming. Rumours circulated that King James had returned at the head of an Irish army and was attacking London in order to conquer it for catholicism. John Verney, who lived in Hatton Garden, described how 'twixt 1 and 2 we were all alarmed by Drums and Bells that the whole Citty and subburbs were up, upon a Report that the Irish were assaulting houses and killing people... all men got to theire arms and lighted Candles in all theire Windows and at their doores, but about 4 or a little after we began to be undeceiv'd and soe went to bed again leaving one or two in a house up'.[13] On that night 10,000 Londoners stood prepared to fight. Sir Robert Geffery, who had been appointed Colonel of the White Regiment in 1681, was among them.

On the day that King James II left London for the last time, 18 December, Prince William of Orange advanced to Westminster, avoiding the crowds. He consulted the Aldermen of the City, their Deputies and Common Councillors promptly and, as the Lord Mayor was incapacitated, Geffery would have been at the forefront of the assembly. On 26 December the Aldermen were again summoned, and by the end of the month Prince William was confident of the support of the City, the peers of the realm and Members of Parliament. There were outbreaks of violence throughout the country but anarchy was averted and in February 1689 William accepted the throne formally and under certain conditions, at a ceremony at Guildhall, which Geffery must have witnessed. King William III of England, Scotland and Ireland and Queen Mary, his wife, hailed as liberators, were crowned the following April. To the relief of Geffery and his Tory Anglican associates, the Bill of Rights (1689) restricted the powers of the monarchy, and the Act of Settlement (1701) assured Anglicans that a Catholic would never again occupy the throne. A revolution had been accomplished and a constitutional monarchy established. The City of London's liberties and franchises had been restored, the Roman Catholic monarch had fled and King William and Queen Mary swore to uphold the Church of England.

SETTLEMENT

The 'old set' of steady Anglican Tory Aldermen had been reinstated by King James II shortly before he left the country in 1688, and these stalwarts provided continuity during the first months of the new reign. The Catholic King and his Catholic agenda having been defeated, the Tory Aldermen looked forward to a period of ascendancy, but for the immediate future the Lord Mayor was a Whig, Sir Thomas Pilkington (1628–91), who held the mayoralty from 1689 until his death in 1691. Pilkington, a merchant and Assistant with the Levant Company, was well-known to Geffery through their mutual trading interests, and they had been political opponents in the 1680s.

With the accession of William and Mary, the tenor of Robert Geffery's life was more settled, but the scope and extent of his responsibilities increased following his appointment as President of Bridewell and Bethlem Hospitals in 1689, a post that required his weekly attendance in the Bridewell court room, sound judgement and a cool head (see chapter 7). In the year of this prestigious appointment, Geffery suffered a personal loss with the death of Sir Henry Tulse. Geffery and Tulse had served the City for decades, shoulder to shoulder, and there was a strong personal bond between them. Tulse left instructions that Geffery should have a suit of 'complete mourning' to wear for the funeral at St

Dionis, Backchurch.[14]

In March 1690 King William demonstrated his confidence in Sir Robert Geffery by appointing him to the Lieutenancy Commission[15] (the Lieutenancy was conferred by the monarch upon those he could trust implicitly to suppress commotions, rebellions and unlawful assemblies). At the same time, Geffery conveyed his personal loyalty to King William by 'loans' of £500 in 1689, and £1,000 in 1690, 1693 and 1694, for the defence of the realm during the war with France.[16] The King had joined the League of Augsburg in 1689, in order to counter French aggression, but the French navy defeated the English and Dutch fleets off Beachy Head in June 1690 and it was another four years before the English fleet made its presence felt in the Mediterranean. The prolonged war was not conducive to trading activities and, in common with other City merchants, Geffery longed for peace (he was still involved with the Levant Company, was an Assistant of the Royal African Company in 1691 and the co-owner of a trading vessel). Whereas he willingly contributed to the cost of the war against France, Geffery did not subscribe to the Bank of England (a Whig enterprise) on its foundation in 1694, although many of his friends did, including Sir William Gore and Captain William Walker.

Geffery continued to serve on the Court of Aldermen throughout King William's reign. He accompanied the Lord Mayor to audiences with the King and was in attendance on ceremonial occasions, the most sombre being the funeral of Queen Mary (who died of smallpox) in December 1694, when the streets of London were draped with miles of black cloth. The Queen's death revived the threat from 'the king across the water' (James II), and a conspiracy to assassinate William came to light in February 1696. His deliverance from plotters and rebels was celebrated by a service of thanksgiving held at St Mary-le-Bow, in Geffery's Ward, in April, followed by a dinner at Ironmongers' Hall.[17] Rumours of plots and Catholic conspiracies were slow to subside and the alarm was raised once again in January 1702 when information was received about a landing of Jacobites on the English coast. King William reacted with severe measures: a royal proclamation ordered all papists and reputed papists to leave London, Westminster, and within ten miles thereof, or face arrest. The proclamation was echoed by the Lord Mayor's 'Precepts against Papists' issued to Aldermen, Churchwardens, constables and City officers. House-to-house searches were ordered, and Alderman Geffery was responsible for compiling lists of the names and places of abode of 'all Papists or Popish recusants or reputed so', whether householders, lodgers or servants, in Cordwainer Ward.[18]

GEFFERY'S HEALTH

The year 1697 brought the first hint of Geffery's age. He pleaded 'old age and infirmities', and requested to be excused from riding in the triumphal procession to welcome King William III into the City on his return from Flanders, following the signing of the Peace of Ryswick,[19] which ended warfare against France for the time being. Geffery suffered a serious illness in August 1700, but by the autumn he was fit enough to participate in meetings of the Court of Aldermen and the Court of the Ironmongers' Company.

In August 1700 it was rumoured that Geffery was 'dyeing in the country, if not dead',[20] (he spent part of each summer in Surrey and must have been taken ill there). However, the old man recovered, returned to his house in Lime Street and was seen leading the Honourable Artillery Company's exercise on 17 September. The mock battle was under his command as the 'General', and his 'enemy' was his friend, 'Lt General' Sir Jeffrey Jeffreys. After Sir Robert had reviewed the troops at the Artillery Ground, the battalion marched to the open fields known as The Baumes, at Hoxton, for an exercise which was described as 'a running fight' in which 'the General' attacked, 'and after springing several mines and carrying the outworks', he led an assault which obliged his besieged adversary 'to beat a parley and surrender'. Thus the members of the Honourable Artillery Company, the country's oldest regiment, 'perfected themselves in field movements', as they continue to do.[21]

Once his health had recovered, Geffery resumed his duties on the Court of Aldermen. The muted piety at Court, the ascendancy of Tories in Parliament and the election of his friend and executor, Sir William Gore as Lord Mayor in 1701, gratified him. Gore's Lord Mayor's Day was the most theatrical for several years, featuring a maiden queen as patroness of the Mercers' Company, and a pageant drawn by nine white horses, three abreast and ridden by 'blackamoors'. Geffery would have been included in the mayoral procession and accompanied Gore to Westminster in the City's barge. The Ironmongers' Company took part in the river procession, aboard a magnificent new state barge, and the Company's liverymen were invited to dine with the Lord Mayor in November. Ironmongers' Hall had recently been renovated and furnished under the supervision of Geffery's committee, and now boasted a music room; the court room had been rebuilt, the windows were reglazed, and the great parlour was furnished with comfortable cane chairs and looking glasses over the mantelpiece, giving the hall touches of luxury in time for Lord Mayor's Day, 1701.[22]

THE ACCESSION OF QUEEN ANNE

The death of King William in the early morning of 8 March 1702 called for an emergency meeting of the Court of Aldermen at Guildhall. As the news spread, the Aldermen made a formal announcement at Temple Bar, proclaiming Queen Anne's accession to the throne. From there the procession of dignitaries proceeded to the Royal Exchange in order to reassure the mercantile community. Before the month was out, Geffery, accompanied by other Aldermen, attended the Queen with the request that she might be 'graciously pleased to do this City the honour to sit for her picture'.[23] Eminent portrait painters were ordered to

OPPOSITE
Queen Anne, soon after
her accession to the throne
in 1702. John Closterman
was commissioned by
the Lord Mayor and
Aldermen to paint her
portrait; this version is
from his studio

prepare sketches: Kneller, Closterman, Richardson and Lentall (Lely was also suggested but he was long dead). John Closterman was awarded the commission and he completed the portrait in 1703.[24]

Stout Queen Anne was the second daughter of King James II, and, like her elder sister, Queen Mary, she had opposed their father's attempt to catholicise England. The Queen and her husband, Prince George of Denmark, were entertained by the Lord Mayor and Aldermen on Lord Mayor's Day in October 1702. Sir William Gore, the outgoing Lord Mayor, and Sir Samuel Dashwood, his successor, contributed £300 each towards the banquet; Geffery and the other Aldermen present gave £50. Queen Anne exerted a moderating influence on domestic politics, but her reign was dominated by the resumption of the war against France. King Louis XIV's aggressive foreign policy and his support for King James II's son, 'The Pretender' to the throne of England, persuaded the House of Commons to declare war in 1702. Geffery did not live to rejoice in the Duke of Marlborough's victory at Blenheim in August 1704, followed by Ramillies (1706), Oudenarde (1708) and Malplaquet (1709), finally leading to the Peace of Utrecht in 1713, which curbed the power of France and laid the foundations of the British Empire.

ENDNOTES

1 *Memoirs of Thomas, Earl of Ailesbury* (1890), vol I, p.175 **2** *The Ellis Correspondence*, ed. G.A. Ellis (1829), vol I, p.244 **3** CMIC, 21 November 1688, GL MS. 16967/7 **4** *The Ellis Correspondence*, op. cit., vol II, p.269. Ellis mistakes the Bucklersbury chapel for the one in Lime Street **5** Dispatches of the Dutch ambassador, 17 November 1688, f.48, Add. MS. 36707, BL **6** Letter Geffery to Sancroft, September 1686, Tanner MS. 142, Bodleian Library, University of Oxford **7** *To His Highness the Prince of Orange. The Humble Address of the Lord Mayor, Aldermen and Commoners of the City of London* (1688) **8** Frances Verney and Margaret M. Verney, *Memoirs of the Verney Family* (1904), vol 3, pp.471 **9** Ibid., pp.469–70. John Verney, later Viscount Fermanagh, who recounted this story, had served his apprenticeship with Gabriel Roberts, Geffery's friend and executor. Verney knew Geffery personally, so may well have heard this account first-hand **10** George Jeffreys's will, 15 April 1689, PRO/PROB11/400, TNA **11** James P. Malcolm, *Anecdotes of the Manners and Customs of London from the Roman invasion to the year 1700* (1811), vol I, p.375, quoting the *English Courant and London Mercury*, 12 December 1688 **12** *The Ellis Correspondence*, op. cit., vol II, pp.350–51 **13** Frances Verney and Margaret M. Verney, op. cit., vol 2, pp.470 **14** Henry Tulse's will, 2 October 1688, PRO/PROB11/394, TNA **15** SPD, March 1690, pp.487, 501. Geffery was re-appointed in 1694, see SPD, February 1694, p.21 **16** *Calendar of Treasury Books 1689–1692*, prepared by W.A. Shaw (1931), vol IX, pt 5, pp.1984, 2004, and vol X, pt I, (1935), pp.16, 910 **17** CMIC, 6 April 1696, GL MS. 16967/7 **18** SPD, 11 January 1702, pp.487–8, and Lord Mayor's Precepts, 20 January 1702, Rep 106 **19** 2 November 1697, Rep 102 **20** Narcissus Luttrell, *A Brief Historical Relation of State Affairs from September 1678 to April 1714* (1857), rev. edn. 1969, vol IV, p.680 **21** James P. Malcolm, *Londinium Redivivum* (1807), vol IV, pp.26–7, quoting *The Protestant Mercury*, 20 September 1700 **22** CMIC, 15 October 1701, GL MS. 16967/7 **23** 26 March 1702, Rep 106 **24** 19 May 1702, Rep 106. The whereabouts of the original portrait is unknown; versions from Closterman's studio can be found at the National Portrait Gallery, London

Sir Robert Geffery Kt

7 | FATHER OF THE CITY

The reign of the despotic King James II had presented Sir Robert Geffery with challenges both political and personal. Riots in the City, repercussions from the Duke of Monmouth's rebellion and, above all, the King's catholicism, caused Geffery grief. After those tempestuous years, the constitutional monarchy of King William III and Queen Mary brought more stable domestic politics, and a few months into the reign, Geffery was appointed President of Bridewell and Bethlem Hospitals, while continuing to serve as Alderman. Within three months of the accession of Queen Anne in 1702, Geffery succeeded Sir John Moore as the senior Alderman, an esteemed position which brought with it the title of Father of the City.[1] This was the zenith of Geffery's forty-three years' dedication to the City of London and he rarely missed a meeting of the Court of Aldermen, dressed in the distinctive grey cloak that indicated he had 'passed the chair', i.e. he was a former Lord Mayor. He made his final appearance at the Court on 3 February 1704, dictated his will a week later and died before the month was out, leaving a generous and lasting legacy.

The last years of Geffery's life tested his stamina. He made his mark as an innovative President of Bridewell and Bethlem Hospitals. He was a revered Past Master of the Ironmongers' Company, which he represented at the Lord Mayor's banquet in 1698, and the following year he was chairing the committee supervising alterations at Ironmongers' Hall.[2] He held a Lieutenancy commission of the City of London, and he accepted the post of Assistant to the Royal African Company for the year 1691–2. He was seen and heard at the Royal Exchange, Guildhall, Ironmongers' Hall, and with his companions at the Bull's Head coffee-house on the corner of Tower Street, and at North's in King Street, Cheapside. Nor was there any let-up in his trading activities, which he expanded by leasing two properties at Leadenhall Market in 1700. In September of the same year his physical energy was such that he commanded an exercise with the Honourable Artillery Company. No less demanding were the annual processions, dinners, services and ceremonies that were an essential part of the City's calendar and at which Alderman Geffery's presence was required.

Geffery's single most important role during the last years of his life was as the President of Bridewell and Bethlem Hospitals from 1689 to 1690 and from 1693 until 1704. In the court room at Bridewell, Geffery dispensed justice every Friday, judging, sentencing or discharging 'distracted' souls, petty criminals and vagrants. His reputation for fairness and his streak of compassion served the Hospitals well. The Governors acknowledged Geffery's exceptional contribution by commissioning his portrait to be painted by Sir Godfrey Kneller, the most famous portraitist of the time.

After Geffery's death in 1704, his will revealed the extent of his philanthropy. He left bequests to alleviate the sufferings of the inmates of London hospitals; poor widows, the poor inhabitants and children of his native village, his parish church, relatives and friends were beneficiaries of his wealth. Above all, he is remembered for his endowment of the Geffrye Almshouses in Shoreditch, now the Geffrye Museum. His desire to provide for almspeople is perpetuated to this day at Geffery's House and Geffery's Fields in Hampshire, where elderly people are housed, while at Landrake, his birthplace, the Sir Robert Geffery School has educated generations of local children.

Bridewell.

A MAN OF STAMINA

In old age Geffery did not shirk the responsibilities that were showered upon him by the Court of Aldermen. None of his contemporaries served that Court and its committees so assiduously and for so long as Geffery (Sir Robert Clayton came close, but his main interest lay in representing the Whigs in Parliament). At a time of national financial crisis, heavy taxation and a decline in the City's revenues, Geffery's advice was sought over the auditing of the Chamberlain's accounts, which revealed that £468 (some £65,000 at 2012 values) had been paid to three clerks of the markets, yet there were no such officers.[3] In 1692 Geffery was appointed a Governor of the Tackle House Porters and Ticket Porters, who loaded, unloaded and carried goods at the port of London;[4] he was on the committee to investigate offences committed by Thames fishermen who netted fish although they were not freemen, so not officially permitted to do so;[5] he was asked to report on encroachments on the river and the state of the City's barges,[6] to inspect the lease of the Southwark court house[7] and to give his opinion about the sale of leather at Leadenhall Market.[8] Alderman Geffery also served on the committee for Emanuel Hospital from 1698 — the school and almshouses had been founded at Tothill Fields, Westminster, in accordance with Lady Dacre's will of 1594 and were incorporated in 1600.[9] Most challenging was the business of the Court of Orphans, which was in a state of financial collapse. Geffery and his committee were tasked with an 'Enquiry for ye relief of ye distressed orphans' of freemen of the City and with petitioning the House of Commons for a Bill to settle the orphans' affairs. Due to the persistence of Geffery and his colleagues over a period of three years,[10] the Court of Orphans was wound up under the Orphans Act of 1694.

In addition to these duties on behalf of the Court of Aldermen, Geffery oversaw the government, policing and administration of Cordwainer Ward from 1676 to 1704. In February 1693 there was a crack-down on 'vice, profaneness and wickedness...unlawful gameing, entertaining lewd women, drunkenness and tippling' on the Lord's Day. Aldermen and constables were commanded to punish anyone who misbehaved in such a fashion on Sundays.[11] As Alderman of a Ward that included Bow Lane, Watling Street and bordered on Cheapside, with eight precincts and eight constables, Geffery must have been busy. Within his Ward, Geffery was authoritarian. As Robert Rogers, Churchwarden of St Mary, Aldermary, discovered, Geffery did not put up with insolence, let alone vice and illegal activities. Geffery instigated proceedings against Rogers, who had insulted him, in January 1702. Consequently, Rogers was summoned to appear before the Common Serjeant, accused of 'menaceing and giving abusive Language' to

Sir Robert Geffery at the Wardmote (a meeting of the citizens of the Ward, presided over by Geffery). The matter was referred to the Court of Aldermen and Rogers was summoned to account for his behaviour. The saga was recorded at length, in Latin, indicating the seriousness of the charge and Geffery's stern reaction to Rogers's insults. Rogers had challenged Geffery's right to hold the Wardmote in the parish of St Mary, Aldermary, without obtaining permission from himself as Churchwarden. So incensed was Rogers that he had insulted Geffery publicly, inferring that Geffery had acted arrogantly: 'You think you are among your Bridewell Birds, you forget yourself,' Rogers had railed, referring to Geffery's position as President of Bridewell and Bethlem Hospitals where he exercised supreme authority (presumably 'Birds' referred to the young women and prostitutes of Bridewell).[12]

PRESIDENT OF BRIDEWELL AND BETHLEM

As an Alderman who had 'passed the chair' (a former Lord Mayor), Geffery was eligible for the presidency of any one of the City's charitable institutions and, in 1689 he was elected President of Bridewell and Bethlem Hospitals. Sir William Turner, a doughty cloth merchant from Yorkshire, had 'laid down his gown' and resigned in November 1688. He was followed briefly by Sir James Smyth, then in July 1689 Sir Robert Geffery was elected President by 'a plurality of hands'.[13]

Bethlem, originally the Priory of St Mary of Bethlehem, was a thirteenth-century foundation situated outside Bishopsgate. Bridewell Palace, west of Blackfriars, had provided the setting for King Henry VIII's divorce proceedings in 1528. Since the mid-sixteenth century Bridewell and Bethlem had been amalgamated in one corporation under the jurisdiction of the City, with one President and a Court of Governors which met weekly. The two institutions fulfilled dual purposes: Bethlem housed lunatics or 'distracted' persons, while Bridewell was primarily a short-term prison for the punishment, discipline and training of vagrants, destitute children, 'strumpets', disobedient servants and 'night-walkers'. Bridewell had been destroyed by the Great Fire of 1666 and rebuilt by Robert Hooke between 1671 and 1678, who also designed the magnificent new Bethlem at Moorfields (1675–6).

It was to the court room at Bridewell that Sir Robert Geffery went every Friday from 1689 to 1690 and from his re-election as President in March 1693 until shortly before his death in February 1704. Ned Ward (1667–1731), alias *The London Spy*, who toured Bridewell in the 1690s, described it as a 'Stately Edifice...rather a Princes' Palace than a House of Correction'. He observed the proceedings taking place in 'A Spacious Chamber where the Court was sitting

N.W. VIEW of the Chapel and Part of the Great Stair-Case leading to the HALL OF BRIDEWELL HOSPITAL, LONDON.

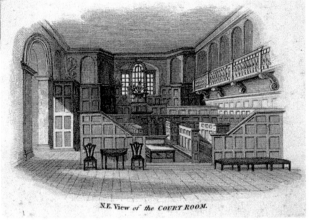

N.E. View of the COURT ROOM.

in great Grandeur and Order. A Grave Gentleman whose Awful Looks bespoke him some Honourable Citizen, was mounted on the Judgement seat, arm'd with a Hammer like a 'Change broker at Lloyds Coffee-House when selling goods by inch of the Candle'. Ward heard the cries of 'a Woman under the lash in the next room' (folding doors in the court room opened into the whipping room), and he watched as another woman, Elizabeth, was brought before the President, Sir Robert Geffery. Having heard that she had been found soliciting, and listened to the evidence of witnesses, Geffery called upon the Court of Governors to make a judgement: 'All you who are willing that E------th T-----ll should have present Punishment, hold up your hands'. Many hands were raised, so Elizabeth was led to the black-draped whipping room where she was forced to bare her back. However, 'The Great Sages of the August Assembly' were so moved by her 'modest mien' and the whiteness of her skin that she received 'but a gentle Correction'.[14]

'GOOD SIR ROBERT'

For nearly twelve years Geffery was that 'Grave Gentleman', described by *The London Spy*, enthroned upon the 'Judgement seat' and presiding over the Governors of Bridewell and Bethlem (among whom stood Sir Gabriel Roberts and Sir William Gore, his executors). In the Bridewell court room some 400 vagrants, indigent and miserable people were brought before Geffery each year. Once judgement was pronounced, they were either discharged, sentenced to transportation, punished and/or imprisoned at Bridewell, or admitted to Bethlem. In this judicial role, Geffery scrutinised each case, as a queue of pick-pockets, petty criminals, 'black Madges' and 'country Besses' of the streets – dissolute and sometimes demented individuals – were brought before him. Francis Lewis, for example, who had stolen two gold rings from his master, was sent by Geffery to the Bridewell workhouse, whereas Susanna Evans, 'a lewd idle and debauched person', was discharged, as was Mary Waite, who was accused of 'living incontinently' with Edward Martin.[15] For the crime of pick-pocketing, a man might be sent 'to sea' (transported overseas), flogging was a common punishment, the stocks and the ducking stool were other means of castigation and prisoners were regularly set to work beating hemp 'in publick view with due correction of whipping'.[16]

One prisoner, William Fuller, wrote an account of his experiences at Bridewell while Geffery was President. Fuller (a friend of the discredited plotter, Titus Oates) was 'convicted for being an Imposter, publishing a false and scandalous libel respecting ministers of the late King William' and several Members of Parliament. With a note detailing his crimes pinned to his hat, Fuller was pilloried, marched to Bridewell and thrown into a dungeon. He managed to obtain 'half a quartern of Brandy' to fortify himself before his appearance before Geffery. 'Sir Robert Jefferies told me that I was sent thither by the Court of Queen's Bench and being ordered to be Whipt, I must undergo that punishment'. Fuller was stripped to the waist, put in the stocks, and Mr Hemings, the whipper, administered thirty-nine 'stripes' with an instrument that had a dozen knotted strings at the end, for thrashing. 'I could not forebear bawling out, but good Sir Robert knockt at last and I was let out of the stocks'; (when the President knocked on the table with the hammer, this signalled a stop to the whipping).[17]

Sir Robert Geffery was sympathetic when Fuller complained of the harsh conditions and vicious inmates at Bridewell, ordering the irons that shackled Fuller to be reduced and allowing him a pen and ink. And when Fuller was nearly bludgeoned to death by the Bridewell hemp-dresser, Mr Waldo, Geffery investigated the affair, summoning Waldo and Fuller before him on 31 July 1702.

He insisted that the injured Fuller be permitted to sit down, and Waldo was ordered to apologise publicly for his violent behaviour. 'Sir Robert promised me Satisfaction and Protection from the like Insults', Fuller reported.[18] Despite his harrowing experiences as a prisoner, Fuller held 'good Sir Robert' in high esteem.

BETHLEM

The lunatics paraded in front of Geffery for judgement were consigned to Bethlem, where they were locked up and sometimes chained in cells which lined the sides of wide galleries. The institution and its inmates were one of the sights of London, attracting visitors, who referred to the place as Bedlam. A previous, dilapidated building had accommodated twenty-five patients and it had earned a reputation for overcrowding, corruption and cruelty. By contrast, the new Bethlem Hospital at Moorfields, designed by Robert Hooke in the 1670s, housed 120 men and women in single cells, behind a facade that influenced the architecture of other London buildings such as the Royal Hospital, Chelsea. 'I think they were Mad that built so costly a Colledge for such a Crack-brained Society', Ned Ward commented when he saw the scale of the new Bethlem.[19]

In its architecture and in its approach to mental illness, Bethlem showed the way, and this was largely due to the enlightened Dr Edward Tyson, physician to the Hospital from 1684 until his death in 1708. Tyson, a churchgoer with Geffery

at St Dionis, Backchurch, was an author, a Fellow of the Royal Society and a Fellow of the Royal College of Physicians. In 1699 he was appointed by Geffery and the Governors to be responsible for the health of prisoners at Bridewell, in addition to the care of lunatics at Bethlem. Tyson was forward-looking in his approach, aiming to alleviate his patients' ailments (many of whom were limbless or suffered from scurvy), and then release them. Tyson and Geffery, physician and President respectively, improved conditions at Bethlem by employing a nurse and by establishing an 'out-patients' facility. Another order enforced during Geffery's presidency disciplined servants working at Bethlem and expelled the lewd and disorderly people who lurked around the place. A more wholesome diet was prescribed for the inmates, giving them meat three times a week, bread, cheese, potage, and fruit in season.[20] By the standards of the time, conditions at Bethlem were good, and were set to improve: 'There is the greatest provision made for them of any Publick charity in the World – if they are not fit to make use of a bed they are provided with fresh clean straw every day', Robert Seymour reported.[21]

Edward Tyson, FRS, FRCP, oil painting by Edmond Lilly, c.1695. Tyson was physician to Bridewell and Bethlem Hospitals during Geffery's presidency

OPPOSITE
Sir William Turner, Lord Mayor 1668–9, oil painting by Mary Beale, 1675. Turner succeeded Geffery as President of Bridewell and Bethlem Hospitals in 1690; Geffery succeeded Turner in 1693

The prisoners of Bridewell and the lunatics of Bethlem were incarcerated and punished if deemed necessary. They also received medical treatment and benefited from rehabilitation. At Bridewell, orphans and destitute children were educated by a reader/schoolmaster and youths were trained – as weavers, tailors or glovers for instance – by 'art-masters' who were retired traders and artisans. As one who had undergone a seven-year apprenticeship and risen to be Master of the Ironmongers' Company, Geffery appreciated the importance of a rigorous training and the opportunities it presented, so he encouraged the training of youths at Bridewell. The 'Bridewell boys' (apprentices) were provided with a uniform of blue and white doublets, breeches and caps, and on completion of their training they were given £10 each to set them on their feet.

At the annual election of the President of Bridewell and Bethlem Hospitals in 1690, Sir Robert Geffery, 'earnestly desiring that he may be dismissed from the said office', proposed that Sir William Turner should replace him (Geffery had his eye on the presidency of St Thomas's Hospital but in this he was to be disappointed). Turner was an experienced President, responsible for commissioning Robert Hooke to design the Bethlem building at Moorfields, and he agreed to serve a second term. Following Turner's death in February 1693, Geffery was elected to succeed him; he agreed and was thanked 'for his worship's soe freely complying with the unanimous desire of this Court'.[22] Almost immediately, the Court of Governors expressed its gratitude by commissioning Geffery's portrait to be painted by either 'Mr Kneller' or 'Mr Lentall'.[23] Sir Godfrey Kneller was chosen and his larger-than-life portrait of Geffery was hung at Bridewell. Three years after Geffery's death, the Governors of Bridewell and Bethlem resolved to enhance the portrait by commissioning 'a new guilt frame att the charge of this Hospital...for the picture of the late right worshipful Sr Robert Jeffereyes in the parlour of this Hospital of Bridewell'.[24]

The Minutes of the Governors of Bridewell and Bethlem Hospitals, 28 April 1693, record 'Sir Robt Geffery to sitt for his Picture'. Following this resolution, Sir Godfrey Kneller was commissioned to paint Geffery's portrait

OPPOSITE
Sir Robert Geffery's portrait by Kneller being hung at Ironmongers' Hall. It was acquired from King Edward's School Witley, in 2008

Not surprisingly, the Ironmongers' Company hankered after a portrait of Geffery, its benefactor, so in 1724 Richard Philips (c.1681–1741), a 'limner', was commissioned to copy the Kneller portrait (he was paid 30 guineas, with 3 guineas going to Mr Denny the frame-maker).[25] Philips's copy hung at Ironmongers' Hall until recently, when the Company negotiated the acquisition of Kneller's original. This had been inherited by King Edward's School (as the school at Bridewell became) and it moved with the school to Witley in Surrey in the mid-nineteenth century. Following negotiations that benefited the Ironmongers' Company and King Edward's School in different ways, it was agreed that the most appropriate home for Kneller's portrait of Geffery was Ironmongers' Hall, where it now dominates the staircase, in its flamboyant baroque frame and surmounted by the subject's heraldic shield.

One of Geffery's first decisions following his election as President in 1693 was to appoint a new minister for Bridewell and Bethlem Hospitals. This was Francis Atterbury (1663–1732) who was at the same time promoted to the post of Chaplain to King William and Queen Mary (Atterbury was a protégé of Henry Compton, Bishop of London, whose dismissal by King James II in 1686 had incensed Geffery and the Anglican stronghold). On Atterbury's election in October 1693, he joined Geffery and the Governors of the Hospitals for a banquet in the great hall at Bridewell. Atterbury was an eloquent preacher whose straightforward, practical Christianity was shared by Geffery, although the latter would not have condoned Bishop Atterbury's later involvement with the Jacobite cause, which forced him into exile. For the meanwhile however, Bridewell and Bethlem were well-served by Geffery as President, Atterbury as preacher and Tyson as physician.

'In the name of God, Amen'

So began the compassionate, thoughtful and charitable will of Sir Robert Geffery, dated 10 February 1703 (1704 according to the modern calendar). The winter had set in at the end of the previous November with a hurricane that destroyed the wondrous Eddystone lighthouse, not far from Geffery's birthplace in Cornwall, while in London 800 houses collapsed due to storm damage, thousands of chimney-stacks fell down and two newly-built turrets on the church of St Mary, Aldermary, in Geffery's Ward, were blown off. The weather continued dark, cloudy and stormy until mid-January. In the first week of February, Geffery took to his bed, nursed by his niece, cared for by 'people washing him in his sickness' and attended by the apothecary, Thomas Gardener, a recent Master of the Society of Apothecaries and a Common Councillor, and Christopher Talman, surgeon to Bridewell and Bethlem Hospitals during Geffery's term as President. [26]

When the Court of the Ironmongers' Company heard of Geffery's declining health, Peter Walker (Master 1699–1700) and Major Thomas Brisco/Briscoe (Master 1710–11) were dispatched to visit the senior member of the Court to convey the Company's respects. Escorted by the Beadle, Walker and Brisco made the pilgrimage to Lime Street in vain, for Geffery was 'soe very ill that att present he was not capable of receiving any Account of the Company's respect for him'. [27]

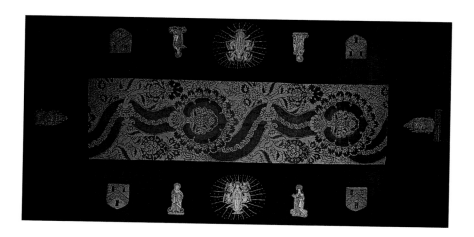

This hearse cloth of 1515, given to the Ironmongers' Company by John Gyva, would most probably have covered Geffery's coffin at his burial, March 1704

Geffery died a week later, on 26 February, aged ninety. On 10 March the Master, Wardens and liverymen of the Ironmongers' Company assembled at their hall in Fenchurch Street to escort Geffery's coffin, draped in the Company's crimson and gold hearse cloth, to the church of St Dionis. Geffery had been devoted to this church 'in which parish through God's mercy I have lived many years';[28] he had served as Churchwarden and had contributed to the cost of rebuilding it after the Great Fire. The funeral service was conducted by the Rector, Lionel Gatford, who had known Geffery for twenty-four years, and it was attended by the Lord Mayor, Sir John Parsons, the Aldermen in their violet mourning gowns, the Master Chamberlain and other City officers marching behind the sword-bearer, who carried the ceremonial sword draped in black. Sir Charles Thorold led members of the Ironmongers' Company (he was the current Master and was to be Geffery's successor as Alderman of Cordwainer Ward); other mourners represented the Levant Company, the Royal African Company and the East India Company. Sir Samuel Dashwood, Sir Gabriel Roberts and Sir William Gore stood among a phalanx of merchants; parishioners Geffery had prayed with and beneficiaries of his will bowed their heads. The deceased had specified that the funeral expenses, mourning gowns and rings should not cost more than £800 (the executors claimed £807, some £100,000 at 2012 values).[29] Accordingly, Sir William Gore, Sir William Russell, Sir Gabriel Roberts and Katherine Geffery (executors), were provided with the traditional black gowns and Alderman Sir Jeffrey Jeffreys and his brother, John Jeffreys, were given mourning rings and £10 each as gestures of affection from their dead friend and business partner.

Unusually, Geffery did not wish his body to be interred alongside his late wife's remains in the chancel of St Dionis. Instead he wanted to be buried in the vault where Sir Henry Tulse's corpse had been placed in 1689, or if this was not possible, 'as near the Communion table as may be'. The Tulse vault was not an option, so by way of a compromise, Geffery's remains were placed within the perimeters of the communion rails, between the two doors on the north side of the chancel. He wanted a monument to be erected in the church 'for myself and my late wife' at a cost of £80 and within weeks of his death his executors applied for permission to place a memorial on the wall, under Geffery's trophies and streamers.[30] Richard Saunders, the carver of Gog and Magog at Guildhall, who had worked for Sir Christopher Wren at All Hallows, Lombard Street, executed the marble monument, for which he was paid £85.[31] In the mid-eighteenth century Geffery's memorial was described as 'a comely Monument erected for him, with eight Penons [pennons, long narrow flags] and a Streamer hanging up near it'.[32] When St Dionis was demolished in 1878, the monument was rescued and erected in the chapel of the almshouses Geffery endowed at

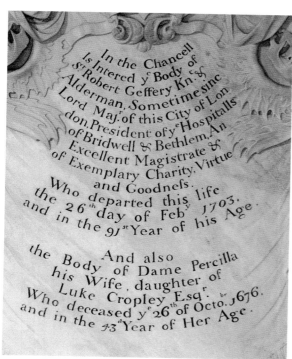

In the Chancell
Is Intered y^e Body of
Sr Robert Geffery Kn^t &
Alderman, Sometime sinc
Lord Maj^r of this City of Lon
don, President of y^e Hospitalls
of Bridwell & Bethlem, An
Excellent Magistrate &
of Exemplary Charity, Virtue
and Goodnefs.
Who departed this life
the 26th day of Feby 1703,
and in the 91st Year of his Age.

And also
the Body of Dame Percilla
his Wife, daughter of
Luke Cropley Esqr.
Who deceased ye 26th of Octo.^{br} 1676,
and in the 43^d Year of Her Age.

Shoreditch. These almshouses closed shortly before the First World War and the monument went with the almspeople to new almshouses at Mottingham in 1913, where it was placed in the entrance corridor. The Mottingham almshouses were sold in 1971 and replaced by Geffery's House at Hook and Geffery's Fields, near Basingstoke, Hampshire. So the monument was returned to the chapel at the former almshouses in Kingsland Road, now the Geffrye Museum.

In his choice of executors, Geffery appointed three 'worthy friends' and his niece, who each received £100 for their pains. Alderman Sir Gabriel Roberts (1629–1715) was a pillar of the Royal African Company, the Levant Company and the East India Company, so he was well acquainted with Geffery's trading interests.[33] Sir William Russell (1643–1705), Past Master of the Skinners' Company, was one of the Aldermen who had been victimised at King James II's whim in 1687, when Geffery had also been dismissed. Russell lived in Gracechurch Street, not far from Geffery's house, and his son was a member of the Ironmongers' Company. Sir William Gore (1644–1708), a Mercer, had been struck out of Geffery's will at some point, then reinstated. The line through his name probably reflected his prosecution for supplying the army and navy with mattresses made of goat, horse and dog hair instead of flock. Gore evidently redeemed himself, for he was one of the original directors of the Bank of England in 1694, Lord Mayor for 1701–2,

OPPOSITE ABOVE
Interior of St Dionis, Backchurch, shortly before demolition in 1878. The monument to Robert and Priscilla Geffery can be seen to the right of the pulpit

OPPOSITE BELOW
The inscription on the monument to Sir Robert Geffery and Dame 'Percilla'

RIGHT
Sir William Gore (1644–1708), Lord Mayor 1701–2 and one of Geffery's executors. Portrait attributed to the school of Sir Godfrey Kneller

and his epitaph testified that he was 'a wise and impartial magistrate, faithful to his prince and useful to his country'.[34] The fourth executor, Katherine Geffery, was a spinster, the third daughter of Robert Geffery's brother, William, who had predeceased him. She lived at Geffery's house in Lime Street and shortly after his death she married John Roberts. Roberts and his family (not to be confused with Lewis, Gabriel and William Roberts who came from Wales) were from Cornwall (see page 23–4). John, his brother Samuel, their four sisters and their widowed mother, Jane Roberts, were all left bequests by Sir Robert Geffery.

Geffery's will opened with a pious, sincere and touching testament to his faith. He commended his soul 'into the hands of Almighty God my Creator and of Jesus Christ my only Saviour by whose mercy and merits I believe and do assuredly hope to obtaine free pardon and remission of all my Sins and Offences and to inherit amongst the Elect the Joyes and fruition of Eternall life. My Body I commit to the Earth from where it was extracted in hope of a joyfull Resurrection at the last day'. His personal devotion to 'the Rubrick and Liturgy of the Church of England' and to his parish church was affirmed by the provision of an allowance to be given to the minister or curate of his parish church, St Dionis, who was instructed to celebrate divine service 'twice every day in the weeke yearly and every year forever' and, practical as ever, Geffery left £50 towards the church's debts.

Geffery's bequests ranged far and wide: family and personal legacies amounted to some £10,350, the largest single portion, £3,000 (the equivalent of some £393,000 at 2012 values), going to his niece Katherine.[35] Several other nieces, their children, his servants, former apprentices and thirty widows of poor Church of England ministers received smaller sums (Geffery specifically directed that money left to women must be paid directly into 'their own hands and noe other'). Cornish connections were not forgotten but personal memories were vague – Geffery did not know if his cousin William of Tremanton or Anne Lower (née Roberts) were living and he had lost contact with his late wife's family, although he conveyed goodwill to widow Cropley by leaving her £20, if she was alive.

A major legacy was to benefit the poor inhabitants and children of Landrake and St Erney in Cornwall, where Geffery had been born and brought up. Firstly, he left instructions that 2 shillings a week was to be 'laid out in bread for the poor Inhabitants', to be distributed every Sunday after divine service (the gift of bread continued until curtailed by agreement in December 1964). Secondly, conscious of the value of an education, Geffery's will specified that a schoolmaster or some such person should be appointed, 'that shall teach the children of the poore Inhabitants within the parishes of Landrake and St Erney aforesaid to write and read English and to learne and be instructed in the Catechisme now used and appointed in the Church of England'. The Master and Wardens of the Ironmongers' Company were endowed with £520 to invest in property to pay for the Landrake charities; similarly the Company was to invest £400 in land or houses to yield an income to pay the Rector of St Dionis to fulfil Geffery's wishes.[36]

Geffery left £400 to Bridewell and Bethlem Hospitals, 'towards the relief of the poor harboured in those hospitalls' and, a personal touch, he gave £5 to Mrs Higgins, the matron of Bridewell.[37] In due course, Geffery's name was inscribed in gold on the list of benefactors on the wall of the Bridewell court room. London's three other hospitals, Christchurch, St Thomas's and St Bartholomew's, received £200 apiece 'towards the relief of the poor harboured therein'. Having been generous to hospitals, his parish church, poor widows, distributed personal bequests, provided for a schoolmaster for the children and bread for the hungry villagers of Landrake and St Erney, Geffery's major endowment was to found almshouses for the elderly poor.

The Geffrye Almshouses

One month after Geffery's death, the Ironmongers' Clerk was in possession of a copy of the will. As he read out the contents, members of the Court were overcome by Geffery's generosity and the extent of their responsibilities as trustees: firstly, the duty of investing in properties to yield the income necessary to fulfil Geffery's wishes and secondly, the administration and maintenance of his benefactions. The priority was to locate and purchase a site to build 'An Almeshouse for soe many poor people as the monies arising by the residuary part of my Estate ...may amount to'. Geffery had clearly given this matter thought. As Master and a longstanding, active member of the Ironmongers, he had been well aware of the number of almspeople who relied on the Company's charity. They were housed in St Nicholas Lane, close to the church of St Nicholas Acons before 1666, and after the Fire, in tenements on the Company's Old Street estate. There were many old, poor people in desperate need, and Geffery's will expressed his earnest resolve to ease the lives of the Ironmongers' almspeople by providing them with a home, an allowance of £6 a year each and 15 shillings each for a gown. While he trusted the Ironmongers to fulfil his wishes, he appreciated the work this would entail, so he left the Company £200, with an additional £30 to buy a pair of silver wine flagons for use at the hall. The Company overspent on the flagons without hesitation,[38] but made little headway in locating a suitable site for the almshouses. Three years after Geffery's death, in May 1707, the committee in charge of his affairs had received £8,500 from the estate and, later that year, the Clerk calculated he had £9,420 in hand for the purchase of land and the building of almshouses thereon.[39] The sum included £3,621 from the sale of several properties; nearly £1,000 (about £131,250 at 2012 values) had been found in ready cash and 'banknotes in his closet'; stocks in various overseas trading companies had been sold, also £234 of orphans stock (as a result of the Orphans Act of 1694 a fund was created for public investment). A quantity of 'oyles' (used in woollen manufacturing or made into soap) in Geffery's possession had been sold for £625 and his 'chariott' and horses went for £54. Plate, jewels and 'household stuff' fetched £408, from which Geffery's debts to the farrier, coachmaker, barber, tailor and brewer were paid.[40]

The search for a site for almshouses took eight years, involving the Ironmongers and Geffery's executors in lengthy negotiations and a case in the Court of Chancery. Part of the problem lay in the deaths of two of the executors, Sir William Russell in 1705, and Sir William Gore in 1708, leaving Sir Gabriel Roberts with heavy responsibilities. Disagreements and negotiations over a suitable site and the hesitant deliberations of the Ironmongers' committee dealing with Geffery's legacies caused delay. Not least of the distractions was the emergence of claimants on Geffery's estate, such as John Lower, 'a poor relation' who needed £3 to be released from Ludgate Prison, and who prayed for further assistance.[41] Another 'near relation', a widow called Madam Jane Cox, turned up at Ironmongers' Hall to demand the £300 Geffery had left her.[42] Edward Dimbleby of Mitcham also put in a claim, averring that Sir Robert and Katherine Geffery, with his coachman and her maid, had lodged with Dimbleby at Mitcham in Surrey, for several summers and that he had been put to 'great charges' in entertaining them. He had received a mere £20 each summer but, he alleged, Geffery 'had often said he would be kind to Dimbleby and his family by will or otherwise'. The executors were inclined to believe Dimbleby, who was on the verge of bankruptcy.[43] They also believed Geffery's clerk, John Southey, who said his late master had promised to propose him for admission to the freedom of the Ironmongers' Company. The Court, 'considering Sir Robert's great affection for the Company', assented.[44]

Sir Gabriel Roberts was Geffery's most conscientious executor. It was he who, in 1705, first directed the Ironmongers' attention to Shoreditch, where some almshouses had recently been built (possibly Aske's Almshouses for the Haberdashers' Company, 1692–5) and where land was available.[45] The Ironmongers' committee favoured a site near Moorfields; the executors objected and the disagreement led to a court case. No wonder that Geffery's niece, Katherine, and her husband, John Roberts, lost patience with the dilatory execution of Geffery's will. Ever since his apprenticeship, Roberts had served Geffery faithfully (one

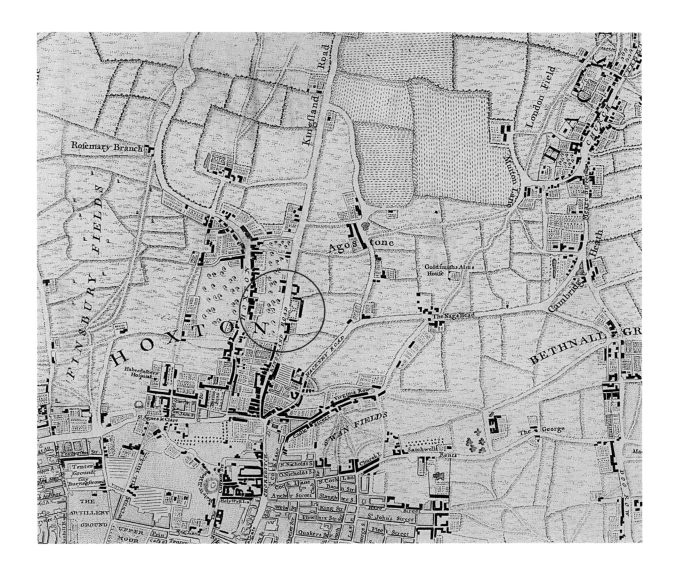

John Roque's map of
1746 shows the site of
the Geffrye Almshouses,
Kingsland Road,
Shoreditch

of his jobs had been to collect his master's dividends in guineas from the Royal
African Company). After Geffery's death, Roberts ensured that a schoolmaster
for the children of Landrake and St Erney was appointed promptly, as Geffery
had directed.[46] Yet by 1707, neither John nor Katherine Roberts, the two people who had been closest to the deceased, had received what was due to them.
Nor had there been any progress in purchasing land for the almshouses which
Geffery had wanted to be built 'with all convenient speed'. The couple tried to
expedite matters, proposing a site for the almshouses in the parish of St Giles,
Cripplegate, but the Ironmongers' committee rejected it.[47]

Following an advertisement placed by the Ironmongers' Company in *The
Postman* of November 1711, Mr Henry Hunt replied with the offer of 'ground
between Shoreditch church and Kingsland, fronting the road'.[48] Ironically, this

was the very same area Gabriel Roberts had pointed to six years earlier. The purchase of the Shoreditch site was completed in 1712 with the payment of £200 to Hunt, and over the next two years, the carpenters Robert Burford and Richard Halsaul, and Mr Strode, the bricklayer, were responsible for the construction of the almshouses, with Burford taking the lead in negotiations with the Ironmongers' Company (he was later employed as the Company's surveyor).[49] On completion of the building in December 1714, sixty-two men and women aged between thirty-eight and eighty applied for residency, although fifty-six was officially the minimum age, and normally the almshouses accommodated between forty and fifty pensioners, each couple or single person in their own room with a fireplace and closet. Housed, and provided with a pension, gown and coal, the ministrations of a chaplain, the services of a doorkeeper and later a matron, the almspeople were well cared for.

Having been home to hundreds of needy, elderly men and women for nearly 200 years, the Geffrye Almshouses were advertised for sale in August 1906. It was claimed that the almspeople were frequently insulted and occasionally assaulted by locals and that the neighbourhood was insalubrious. Fortunately, the proposed sale of the almshouses to the Peabody Trust for redevelopment was averted by strong objections led by the National Trust, the Society for the Protection of Ancient Buildings and the Metropolitan Public Gardens Association. The latter was especially anxious to prevent the loss of the gardens, which formed an oasis adjacent to the noisy, busy, dirty Kingsland Road, in an area that was then the second most densely populated district of London. The local Member of Parliament and the Medical Officer for Shoreditch bolstered

A view of the Geffrye Almshouses in 1805, artist unknown. The watercolour was presented to the Ironmongers' Company by Rev. John Gerrard, Chaplain to the Almshouses

OPPOSITE
View of the Almshouses and front garden, 1906

the case for the preservation of the gardens (two large lawns, a small pond and ancient trees fronting the buildings and to the rear a narrow strip of back yards running the entire length of the almshouses). The London County Council stepped in, agreeing to purchase the almshouses and gardens from the Peabody Trust in December 1910 for £34,289 (part of which was raised by Shoreditch Metropolitan Borough Council and a smaller amount by voluntary subscriptions). Thus the early-eighteenth-century buildings were neither destroyed nor vandalised but were preserved, and the front gardens, which had been planted with ninety lime trees in 1719, were opened to the public in July 1912. The LCC had also purchased numbers 21–61 Maria Street, which were demolished to make way for a children's playground to the rear of the almshouses, now gardens. That settled, the future role of the redundant almshouses remained controversial. An influential consortium of architects and conservationists (Halsey Ricardo, Edwin Lutyens and Richard Norman Shaw among them) weighed in, campaigning for a museum and exhibition room for the arts and crafts, and the LCC responded positively. What emerged was a proposal for a museum of furniture and woodwork, an original concept that reflected the skills and trades of Shoreditch. In the event however, the museum opened in April 1914 and its early displays were mixed, including furniture and panelling but also other material such as metalwork and ceramics.

While the debate about the future of the almshouses raged, the almspeople moved out of Shoreditch to a more peaceful haven at Mottingham Park, Eltham, where a new building was designed by the Ironmongers' surveyor, George Hubbard (1912–14). By the 1970s, that building, which had been bombed during the Second World War, needed modernisation. It was decided to sell rather than renovate, so the almspeople were transferred to newly-built flats named after their benefactor, Geffery's House at Hook (1976), supplemented by Geffery's Fields at Basingstoke (1984). Faithful to Sir Robert Geffery's will, the Ironmongers' Company continues to administer these almshouses.

GEFFERY'S LEGACY

400 years after Sir Robert Geffery's birth, he is remembered and celebrated for his philanthropy. His presence looms over the staircase at Ironmongers' Hall where the Kneller portrait is displayed, and in the garden of the almshouses at Hook a fine statue of Geffery by John Nost the younger presides. In 1724 Nost was paid £40 for his 'hard metall' statue, designed for the niche above the entrance to the chapel of the almshouses in Kingsland Road, Shoreditch, (the fee included the provision of a polychrome model which the Ironmongers wanted to display at their hall).[50] On the removal of Nost's statue to the almshouses at Mottingham, and from there to Geffery's House at Hook, it was replaced by the replica which greets visitors to the Geffrye Museum; underneath it, an inscription calls attention to 'Sr Rob Geffryes Knt Alderman and Ironmonger Founder of this Hospitall'.[51] A stone's throw away, in the north-west corner of the front garden, the remains of Sir Robert and Priscilla, rescued from St Dionis, Backchurch, on its demolition in 1878, have been laid to rest on land that was purchased in 1716 for the Ironmongers' graveyard.[52] Here the Gefferys' monolithic granite tomb forms the centrepiece, dominating the modest graves and memorials to others associated with the Ironmongers' Company and the almshouses: Thomas Betton, the wealthy Turkey merchant/Ironmonger who died in 1724, Mrs Mary Cook (d. 1747, the widow of an Ironmonger) and her daughter, the Rev. William Hesse, Chaplain to the almspeople (d. 1792), and Mrs Marie Chapman (d. 1840), a devoted matron.

Hundreds of miles away, at Geffery's birthplace in Cornwall a finely-wrought slate panel on the wall of St Michael's Church, Landrake, is inscribed with the clause from Geffery's will detailing his bequest to the inhabitants of Landrake and St Erney, which paid for a schoolmaster for the children and bread for the poor on Sunday. At the other end of Landrake village stands the Sir Robert Geffery Church of England Primary School, which developed from the employment

Assembly at the Sir Robert Geffery School, Landrake, Cornwall, 1888

The Sir Robert Geffery Church of England Primary School, Landrake. Geffery's will of 1704 left money to provide for a schoolmaster for the poor children of Landrake and St Erney. A school opened in 1881; this shows the new school building. Plaques on the wall (right) record that the foundation stone was laid by Robert Stedall, Master of the Ironmongers' Company, in 1989. The site was the gift of the Earl of Mount Edgcumbe

of the first schoolmaster in 1704 and the building of the first school in 1881. Geffery's name is also perpetuated by the Geffery Memorial Hall and Geffery Close, Landrake; by Geffery's Close, London SE9 (formerly the Mottingham almshouses), by Geffrye Street, Geffrye Court, the Geffrye Estate and of course by the Geffrye Museum, Shoreditch.

Sir Robert Geffery, twice Master of the Ironmongers' Company, Sheriff, Alderman and Lord Mayor, Assistant of the Royal African Company, trader with the East India Company and the Levant Company, ship-owner, President of Bridewell and Bethlem Hospitals, Governor of the Irish Society, Churchwarden and philanthropist was, as the list indicates, renowned. The monarch, ministers of state, merchants, politicians and lawyers respected his honesty, integrity, fairness and faith. His personal qualities and not, as was often the case, aristocratic connections or wealth, accounted for his successful career. Loyal, dutiful and hard-working, Geffery made his mark among the merchant community, while at the same time attending to the needs of poor parish children, quelling riots at the Lime Street 'mass-house' and defending his actions to King James II. With the confidence of a self-made man, Geffery held his own in London society and politics, and revelled in the ceremony and pageantry of the City. The youth who arrived in the capital from Cornwall in 1629 or 1630 was, fifty-six years later, The Rt Hon. The Lord Mayor of London, an achievement that speaks of soaring ambition and relentless application. The major breakthrough for young Geffery was his apprenticeship to Richard Peate, Master of the Ironmongers' Company in 1630. Membership of this Company, the tenth of the 'Great Twelve' City livery companies, and his marriage to the eldest daughter of a wealthy member of the Mercers' Company, the premier livery company, paved the way to the mayoralty. As a liveryman, and later Master of the Ironmongers, Geffery had access to City politics and trading opportunities. These he grasped.

Both the diarist Samuel Pepys and Lord Chancellor Jeffreys found Robert Geffery good company. He could down flagons of wine, subdue a riot and he was not intimidated by King James II. He liked the trappings of office, kept a coach and horses and decked his table with silver. Ostentatious perhaps, but unsophisticated, and a man whose simple faith was not shaken by the religious and political vicissitudes of the seventeenth century. The elaborate monument to Sir Robert and Dame 'Percilla' (Priscilla), originally at St Dionis Backchurch and now at the Geffrye Museum celebrates Geffery's career and pays homage to one who served the City of London and its people for half a century and through perilous times: 'Sir Robert Geffery, Knt & Alderman, Sometime since Lord Mayr of this City of London, President of ye Hospitalls of Bridewell & Bethlem. An Excellent Magistrate & of Exemplary Charity, Virtue and Goodness'.

OPPOSITE
Monument to Robert and Priscilla Geffery, now in the chapel at the Geffrye Museum. It was executed by Richard Saunders between 1704 and 1707 at a cost of £85

ENDNOTES

1 Geffery is omitted from the list of Fathers of the City compiled by A.B. Beaven in *The Aldermen of the City of London* (1908–13). Beaven pointed out the difficulty of making a satisfactory list. Strictly speaking the title was given to the senior i.e. the oldest Alderman and in 1702 this was Geffery. Sir Robert Clayton (born in 1629) became Father of the City on Geffery's death in 1704 2 CMIC, 27 April 1699, GL MS. 16967/7 3 26 April 1692, Rep 96. Figures derived from E.H. Phelps Brown and Sheila V. Hopkins, 'Seven centuries of the prices of consumables compared with builders' wage rates', *Economica*, November 1956, and the UK Retail Price Index 2012, www.wolfbane.com/rpi 4 CMIC, 16 February 1692, GL MS. 16967/7 5 20 October 1692, Rep 96 6 23 June 1692, Rep 96, and 9 February 1693, Rep 97 7 Ibid., 12 January 1693 8 8 June 1697, Rep 101 9 In 1623 on the death of Lady Dacre's last surviving executor, the guardianship of Emanuel Hospital passed to the Lord Mayor and Aldermen of the City 10 13 November, 12 December 1691, Rep 96 11 14 February 1693, Rep 97 12 30 June 1702, Rep 106 13 Bridewell Royal Hospital, Minutes of the Court of Governors, 9 July 1689, www.bethlemheritage.org.uk/archive. Geffery's friend, Sir Henry Tulse, had been elected first but begged to be excused (he died the next month). Sir Patience Ward, Sir John Smyth and Geffery were then nominated and Geffery gained the most votes 14 Ned Ward, *The London-Spy Compleat* (1700), rev. edn. 1924, pp.136, 141 15 Bridewell Royal Hospital Minutes, op. cit., 21 January 1704 16 Robert Seymour, *A Survey of the Cities of London and Westminster, Borough of Southwark and parts adjacent* (1734), vol I, p.185 17 *William Fuller's Trip to Bridewell* (1703), pp.2, 8, 9 18 Ibid., p.26 19 Ned Ward, op. cit., p.62 20 John Strype, *A Survey of the Cities of London and Westminster and the Borough of Southwark* (1754), vol I, p.221 21 Robert Seymour, op. cit. 22 Bridewell Royal Hospital Minutes, op. cit., 7 April 1693 23 Ibid., 28 April 1693. Lentall/Lenthall painted the second and third wives of John Verney, Viscount Fermanagh, Geffery's associate in the Royal African Company 24 Bridewell Royal Hospital Minutes, op.cit., 7 March, 1707 25 CMIC, 19 November 1724, GL MS. 16967/9 26 Executors' Accounts (1707) record payments to Gardener, Talman and servants, C9/332/55, TNA 27 CMIC, 18 February 1704, GL MS. 16967/7 28 Geffery's will, 10 February 1704, PRO/PROB11/475, TNA, is the source for the following quotations unless stated otherwise 29 Phelps Brown and Hopkins Index and UK Retail Price Index 2012, see note 3 above 30 St Dionis Vestry Minutes, 29 March 1704, Ms. 4216/2, LMA 31 Executors' Accounts, op. cit. The carver is sometimes referred to as Captain Saunders 32 John Strype, op.cit., p.477 33 Gabriel Roberts was godfather to Martha Evelyn, granddaughter of the diarist John Evelyn

In the Chancell
is Interred y^e Body of
Sr Robert Geffery Kn^t &
Alderman, Sometime sine
Lord Ma:^r of this City of Lon
don, President of y^e Hospitalls
of Bridwell & Bethlem, An
Excellent Magistrate &^c
of Exemplary Charity, Virtue
and Goodnes.
Who departed this life
the 26th day of Feby 1703.
and in the 91th Year of his Age.

And also
the Body of Dame Percilla
his Wife, daughter of
Luke Cropley Esqr.
Who deceased ye 26th of Octo. 1676.
and in the 33th Year of Her Age.

REMOVED A.D. 1915 FROM SIR ROBERT GEFFERY'S ALMSHOUSE
KINGSLAND ROAD WHERE HIS TOMB REMAINS RETURNED 1976

34 Perry Gauci, *The Politics of Trade. The overseas merchant in trade and society 1609–1720* (2001), p.89 35 Phelps Brown and Hopkins Index and UK Retail Price Index 2012, see note 3 above 36 On the demolition of St Dionis in 1878 the legacy was transferred to Bridewell and Bethlem Hospitals 37 Geffery's will, op. cit. 38 The flagons, valued at £49 11shillings, are listed on inventories 1704–1737/8, GL MS.16988/9. Thereafter, inventories are sketchy, especially during the rebuilding of Ironmongers' Hall (1745–50) and there are no further references to Geffery's flagons 39 CMIC, 17 July 1707, GL MS. 16967/8 40 Executors' Accounts, op. cit. 41 CMIC, 30 April 1706, GL MS. 16967/8 42 9 August 1705, Geffery's charity minute book, GL MS. 17052 43 CMIC, 9 August 1705, 21 June 1706, GL MS. 16967/8 44 Ibid., 7 April 1704, GL MS. 16967/7 45 Ibid., 9 August 1705, GL MS. 16967/8 46 Ibid., 23 November 1704, GL MS. 16967/7. A John Roberts, possibly a son of John Roberts junior, was appointed Governor and Chief Agent for the Royal African Company at Cape Coast Castle in 1749, T70/1467, TNA 47 Ironmongers' Company v. Roberts, 1707, C9/332/55, TNA 48 CMIC, 7, 20 March 1711, GL MS. 16967/8 49 Burford may have been the Robert Burford who worked for Wren at Hampton Court Palace in the 1690s, see Neil Burton, *The Geffrye Almshouses* (1979), pp.22–3. The site purchased from Hunt and Richard Longford was 390 feet north to south, 187 feet east to west 50 CMIC, 21 November 1723, 20 January 1724, GL MS. 16967/9. The model is presently in the Clerk's office, Ironmongers' Hall 51 Included in Nost's fee was the model for the statue, which the Ironmongers' Company wished to retain, CMIC, 21 November 1713 and 20 January 1724, GL MS. 16967/8 and /9. Described as the 'small statue' it was placed in the drawing room at Ironmongers' Hall, Fenchurch Street in 1750, later in the court room (see Nicholl pp.452–3) and is now in the Clerk's office at the hall. The replica of the full-size statue at the Geffrye Museum was made by Messrs James Maude and Co (1912) 52 The site comprised 20 feet facing the main road, a width of 38 feet to the east, and a depth of 187 feet, see London County Council, *The Survey of London vol viii. The Parish of St Leonard Shoreditch* (1922), p.128

A polychrome lead figure of Sir Robert Geffery. A model for the larger statue by John Van Nost the younger, 1724

OPPOSITE
View of the Geffrye Museum, 2006. A replica of Nost's statue of Geffery is in the niche above the door

SELECT BIBLIOGRAPHY

GENERAL

Alfred B. Beaven,
*The Aldermen of the City
of London* (1908–13)

Walter Besant, *London in the
time of the Stuarts* (1903)

William Chancellor, *Some
Account of the several wards,
precincts and parishes in the
City of London* (1772)

Christopher Clapham,
*Index to the Freedom Books
of the Worshipful Company
of Ironmongers* (1977)

Edward Hatton, *A New
View of London* (1708)

*Oxford Dictionary of
National Biography* (2004)

Reginald R. Sharpe, *London
and the Kingdom* (1894)

John Stow(e), *The Survey
of London* (1598), rev. edn.
C.L. Kingsford (1943)

John Strype, *A Survey of
the Cities of London and
Westminster* (1754)

*The Corporation of London.
Its Origin, Constitution,
Powers and Duties* (1950)

J.R. Woodhead, *The Rulers
of London 1660–89* (1965)

CHAPTER 1

George C. Boase, and
William P. Courteney,
*Bibliotheca Cornubiensis.
A Catalogue of the writings
relating to the County of
Cornwall* (1874)

Mary Coate, *Cornwall in
the Great Civil War and
Interregnum 1642–1660* (1933)

H.L. Douch (ed.),
*The Cornwall Muster Roll
1569* (1984)

Anne Duffin, *Faction and
faith: politics and religion of
the Cornish gentry before the
Civil War* (1996)

E.A. Fry (ed.), *Calendar of
Wills and Administrations
relating to the Counties of Devon
and Cornwall proved in the
Consistory Court of the Bishop
of Exeter 1532–1800* (1914)

Davies Gilbert, *The Parochial
History of Cornwall* (1838)

J. Polsue, *A Complete
Parochial History of the County
of Cornwall* (1868)

T.L. Stoate, *Cornwall Hearth
and Poll Taxes 1660–64*
(1981), and *The Cornwall
Military Survey 1522* (1987)

J.L. Vivian and H.H. Drake
(eds.), *The Visitation of the
County of Cornwall in the year
1620* (1874)

CHAPTER 2

J. Adams Beck, *The
Ironmongers' Company.
An Historical Note* (1954)

Corporation of London,
*Analytical Indexes to the
series of records known as
the Remembrancia preserved
among the archives of the City
of London 1579–1664* (1878)

William Chancellor, *Some
Account of the several wards,
precincts and parishes in the
City of London* (1772)

T.C. Dale, (ed.),
*The Inhabitants of London
in 1638* (1931)

Elizabeth Glover, *A History
of the Ironmongers' Company*
(1991)

Harleian Society, *Registers of
St Dionis Backchurch London
1538–1754* (1838)

Philip E. Jones, (ed.),
The Fire Court (1966)

Keith Lindley, *Popular Politics
and Religion in Civil War
London* (1997)

W. Niven, *London City
Churches destroyed since
1800AD* (1887)

Peter Mills and John Oliver,
*The Survey of Building Sites
in the City of London after the
Great Fire of 1666* (1967)

Valerie Pearl, *London and
the Outbreak of the Puritan
Revolution* (1961)

Thomas. F. Reddaway,
*The Rebuilding of London
after the Great Fire* (1940,
1951)

C. Webb, *London Apprentices.
Ironmongers' Company
1655–1800* (1999)

Charles Wilson, *England's
apprenticeship 1603–1763*
(1965)

Wren Society, *The Parochial
Churches of Sir Christopher
Wren 1666–1718*, vol IX (1932)

CHAPTER 3

Kenneth R. Andrews, *Trade, Plunder and Settlement. Maritime enterprise and the genesis of the British Empire 1480–1630* (1984)

Robert Brenner, *Merchants and Revolution. Commercial Change, Political Conflict and London's Overseas Traders 1550–1653* (1993)

K.N. Chaudhuri, *The Trading World of Asia and the English East India Company 1660–1760* (1978)

Philip D. Curtin, *The Atlantic Slave Trade* (1969)

K.G. Davies, *The Royal African Company* (1957)

Ralph Davis, 'English Foreign Trade 1660–1700', *Economic History Review*, series 2, vol VII (1954), pp.150–166

Anthony J. Farrington, *Catalogue of East India Company Ships' Journals and Logs 1600–1834* (1999)

Perry Gauci, *The Politics of Trade. The overseas merchant in trade and society 1660–1720* (2001)

Richard Grassby, *The business community of seventeenth-century England* (1995)

Rowan Hackman, *Ships of the East India Company* (2001)

Hugh Johnson, 'Nicholas Leate (1659–1635)', *The Worshipful Company of Ironmongers' Annual Report* (2010–11), pp.6–7

John Keay, *The Honourable Company. A History of the East India Company* (1991)

Margaret Makepeace, (ed.), *Trade on the Guinea Coast 1657–1666. The Correspondence of the English East India Company* (1991)

Russell Miller, *The East Indiamen* (1980)

CHAPTER 4

Charles Carlton, *The Court of Orphans* (1974)

Gary S. De Krey, *London and the Restoration 1659–1683* (2005)

A. Charles Knight, *Cordwainer Ward in the City of London. Its History and Topography* (1917)

Liza Picard, *Restoration London* (1997)

Jenny Uglow, *A Gambling Man. Charles II and the Restoration 1660–1670* (2009)

C. Goold Walker, *The Honourable Artillery Company 1537–1947* (1954)

Brian Weiser, *Charles II and the Politics of Access* (2003)

CHAPTER 5

Robin Clifton, *The Last Popular Rebellion. The Western Rising of 1685* (1984)

Mireille Galinou, (ed.), *City Merchants and the Arts 1670–1720* (2004)

Valerie Hope, *My Lord Mayor. Eight Hundred Years of London's Mayoralty* (1989)

Betty R. Masters, *The Public Markets of the City of London surveyed by William Leybourn in 1677* (1974)

CHAPTER 6

Maurice Ashley, *The Glorious Revolution of 1688* (1966)

R. Brenner, *Merchants and Revolution* (1993)

Tim Harris, *Revolution. The Great Crisis of the British Monarchy 1685–1720* (2006),

Mark Knights, 'A City Revolution. The Remodelling of the London Livery Companies in the 1680s', *English Historical Review*, vol CXII, no 449 (1997), pp.1141–78

Steve Pincus, *1688. The First Modern Revolution* (2009)

William L. Sachse, 'The Mob and the Revolution of 1688', *Journal of British Studies*, vol IV, no 1 (1964), pp.23–40

W.S. Singer, (ed.), *The Correspondence of Henry Hyde, Earl of Clarendon and of his brother Laurence Hyde, Earl of Rochester* (1828)

CHAPTER 7

Jonathan Andrews, Asa Briggs, Roy Porter, Penny Tucker, Kier Waddington, *The History of Bethlem* (1997)

Neil Burton, *The Geffrye Almshouses* (1979)

Kathy Haslam, *A History of the Geffrye Almshouses* (2005)

Edward G. O'Donoghue, *The Story of Bethlehem Hospital* (1914), and *Bridewell Hospital. Palace, Prison, Schools* (1923–9)

L.C.C., *Survey of London* vol VIII. *The Parish of St Leonard Shoreditch* (1922)

London Record Society, *London Inhabitants within the Walls 1695* (1966)

Robert Seymour, *A Survey of the Cities of London and Westminster, Borough of Southwark and Parts Adjacent* (1734)

Craig Spence, *London in the 1690s. A Social Atlas* (2006)

INDEX

ABOUT THE AUTHOR

Penelope Hunting graduated with an honours degree in
history from the University of London, followed by a PhD in
architectural history (1979). She has written numerous books
on the history and development of London, its institutions and
the City livery companies. Her *History of the Royal Society of
Medicine* (2002) received the Society of Authors' award, and she
has recently written a monograph about Cardinal Newman and
his circle. Dr Hunting is a Fellow of the Society of Antiquaries,
Chairman of the London Topographical Society and sits on
the editorial board of the *Journal of Medical Biography*.